In Pursuit of the Perfect Paella

(Further adventures from a new life in Spain)

Mark Harrison

Copyright © Mark Harrison 2019
Mark Harrison has asserted his right under the Copyright, Designs and Patents Act 1988 to be identified as the author of this work.
This book is sold subject to the condition that it shall not, by way of trade or otherwise, be lent, resold, hired out, or otherwise circulated without the author's prior consent.

Author's Note
The anecdotes in this book are based on true events but there is no guarantee of accuracy. Names of characters and places may have been changed to protect privacy. All the characters in this book are to be considered fictional, and any resemblance to actual persons, living or dead, is purely coincidental.

This book is a sequel to *I Want to Live in Spain* first published in 2004 and republished as an eBook in 2013 and as a paperback in 2019.

For Vivien and for Ben and for our beloved Jessie.

Chapter One

(Location – the Jalon Valley situated in the Northern Costa Blanca about twelve miles inland from the City of Denia and the resorts of Javea, Moraira and Calpe. It is half an hour from Benidorm and one hour from Alicante airport. The town of Jalon itself is gradually becoming better known by its Valencian name of Xaló since an official name change was adopted by the local council.)

The memory of that gin and tonic, its juniper hints chilled over solid rocks of ice, was still fresh in my mind. The effervescent liquid tantalised my taste buds and satiated the craving I had harboured for almost a year. It had taken that long for my newly planted lemon tree to flower and bear fruit. I had feared that Vicente, the man at the local agricultural cooperative who sold me the specimen, was right when he told me it would be three years before the tree would bear fruit. Determined to prove him wrong, I had nurtured the sapling with copious quantities of water and liquid fertilizer especially recommended for citrus trees. I watched the first flush of flowers emerge from tight pink buds and cheered at the sight of numerous bees anxious to sample the nectar and aid the process of pollination.

Almost daily, I inspected the foliage looking for evidence of leaf-curl and pinching out affected fronds. Regular spraying with insecticide to ward off fruit flies would surely guarantee an abundant crop. Downhearted, despondent, dejected, I watched as each of the flowers gradually withered and died without producing fruit. Perhaps Vicente was right and I would have to be more patient – never a strong suit in the amalgam of traits that make up my persona. And then I spotted it – a single tiny lemon, green in colour and about the size of a pea, clinging to life at the end of a branch. That was in the spring time, now it was October and though it was barely ripe, my impatience could no longer be held in check. I plucked the fruit and attacked it with my sharpest knife, producing the perfect slice to drop in the glass with a satisfying plink. Combined with the oily infusion of Gordon's gin and Schweppes tonic water, the sharpness of the lemon's flesh and the aromatic zing of the zest produced what must surely have been the best gin and tonic ever made. It buoyed my spirits and satisfied my inner soul, convincing me that there was no better place to be than here in Spain in our little villa on the outskirts of the mountain village of Parcent, just a stone's throw from the Costa Blanca.

It was now just over two years since Viv and I took the momentous decision to quit our jobs and our house in leafy Surrey in order to pursue a more tranquil and less stressful life in Spain. We were never really sure what to expect since our decision had been taken rather rashly and, in my case, with a degree of impetuosity. I still marvelled at the trust Viv had placed in my judgement when I persuaded her that we should buy Casa Emelia even though she had never seen the place. But that impetuosity carried with it a degree of responsibility, albeit self-imposed, to secure our future happiness and well-being. It was a responsibility that, at times, would become a heavy burden to shoulder.

Sure we expected the sunshine for which the Costa Blanca is renowned, and it didn't disappoint in delivering the promised three hundred days a year. The trouble was that at least sixty of those days were too hot, inducing indolence and boredom, not to mention a little irritability. And sixty were too cold, inducing wistful thoughts of fitted carpets, double glazing and central heating, especially when the novelty of lighting a log fire and clearing the ash had worn off. But, hey, that still left eight months of the year when the weather was, well, pretty much perfect. We even learned to love the rain when it came, usually in torrential downpours, to refresh the garden, replenish the aquifers and give us a good excuse to get on with those tasks which we deliberately put back for a rainy day. More than anything though, we had grown accustomed to blue skies and light levels that illuminated our garden and the surrounding mountains, banishing memories of those endless dull days in England when daylight seemed but a fleeting moment, and when everything appeared unremittingly grey, dark and damp.

So we began to adjust, not only to the climate, but to our new surroundings as well. Our beloved German shepherd, Jessie, made her own adjustments and, in truth, had done so without any signs of rueful reflection. I put that down, as I often told Viv, to the fact that dogs don't have long term memories and, as their lives are generally governed by the whims of their owners, they are spared the luxury of harking back to previous times and wondering "what if?"

Unfortunately, the same cannot be said of us humans. As much as we tried to convince ourselves that we had made the right lifestyle choice in swapping our frenetic existence in England for the leisurely placidity of life in Spain, there were moments when we both questioned the wisdom of our move. Usually this was when confronted with the language barrier (something we were still working to resolve) or when challenged by the seemingly impenetrable wall of Spanish bureaucracy, or the idiosyncratic nature of public utilities, or the regular frustrations of the *mañana* culture which is inherent in the Spanish psyche.

It seemed we weren't alone in accommodating these occasional feelings of discontentment. Some of the acquaintances we made on arrival in Parcent – including some of those almost insufferably smug people who in the early days gloated about their wisdom in abandoning Britain since it was "going to the dogs" – had now transmuted into inveterate moaners. Now they frequently donned their red, white and blue tinted spectacles to complain about the irritations of Spanish life and lament the things they missed "back home."

Although I admit to sporadic lapses into misty-eyed nostalgia for that "green and pleasant land," I was always capable of rationalising my circumstances. It never took me very long to convince myself that I had made the right choice. Viv was not always so easily convinced, especially in the height of summer when a dozen weeks of relentless heat reduced her to a state of soggy, sticky, irritable distress. She was not alone, for what had started as a casual observation, became confirmed in fact – women cope less well (to put it mildly) with the heat than men. For me and most of the (expat) men I met, sweating was simply the body's natural way of cooling down. Sweating was good; it cleansed the pores and released all those nasty toxins, and it was easily counteracted by a cold shower or a languid swim in the pool at the end of a morning's labour. For Viv, and for most of the women with whom she frequently compared notes, sweating was uncomfortable, disgusting, irritating, unhygienic. And that irritability led on occasions to bouts of prickly petulance and, to my mind, irrational thoughts of returning to Blighty. Mosquito bites (which were never suffered in the UK) only inflamed the problem, as did stuffy bedrooms, noisy fiestas, a diet based on lettuce and enforced torpidity. I soon learned to recognise the onset of these symptoms and to steer clear of any subject that might provoke Viv into a bout of gratuitous melancholy.

I could have waxed lyrical about the privileged existence we enjoyed – breakfasting on the terrace for six months of the year, being serenaded by the crickets as we lingered outdoors in the fresh evening air, swimming before breakfast, snoozing shirtless in the winter sun, barbequing in January, the absence of traffic jams, the friendliness of the locals, the cost of living, dispensing with socks (I could go on – and on). But the truth was, that at the height of summer, Viv would have no truck with my judicious attempts at mollification. So I learned to stay quiet – or just keep out of the way. Small wonder we both looked forward to September – though for entirely different reasons.

When it was too hot to work, I forced myself to persevere in my efforts to learn Spanish. I hated languages as a schoolboy (German and French 'O' Levels, both failed) and I convinced myself that I just didn't have a flair for foreign tongues. Now, I realised that all I had lacked was motivation. And with that motivation I had little difficulty spending an hour or so every day pouring through the pages of a book called "501 Spanish Verbs" (fully conjugated in all the tenses in an easy to learn format – so the cover said). At times I tore my hair out over the *imperfecto* and the *pretérito*, not to mention the *imperetivo* and the *subjuntivo*, but gradually some of it began to sink in. An "advanced" (sic) Spanish course expanded my vocabulary and I began to feel I had broken through a glass ceiling of sorts. Now I could talk to Spaniards on all manner of subjects rather than just about the weather. My Spanish was still patchy, but people generally understood me (or at least pretended to) though I still had to punctuate most conversations with, *'Lo siento, mas despacio por favor.'* (Sorry, more slowly please). I realised, then, that the average Spaniard is incapable of speaking slowly for more than a sentence or two before reverting to rapid fire delivery. This usually meant my brain was a few seconds (or minutes) behind, still struggling to decipher the sentence before last.

Viv had more sense. Having reached a level where she felt she could get by in most situations, she decided she was too old to return to school and get bogged down with homework. Me? I refused to accept that youth had an advantage over age, and what my memory circuits lacked in capacity and processing power was more than countered by enthusiasm and resolve.

It would take an earthquake to shift me from my unshakeable belief that we had landed, perhaps more by good luck than by good planning, in Avalon. And an earthquake we experienced one morning as a steady tremor rattled the pots and ornaments and rippled the pool for a couple of minutes before gradually subsiding. 'It's nothing to worry about,' our Spanish neighbour, Rosa, explained. 'The mountains are quite young and they are still settling down.'

But it was an earthquake of a different kind that was to rock my confidence and shatter my sanguinity.

I had just finished the final edits on my first book when a neighbour called round with bad news. 'They're going to put a road through my garden.' she said.

I had heard so many rumours about developments planned for our area that I was sceptical about this latest alarm. But Tina had heard the news direct from the town hall. She had been there to ask about permission to construct a swimming pool, only to be told that this was out of the question because a plan had been submitted to finish our urbanisation and build more houses around our little enclave. There would be new roads, footpaths, street lighting and sewers to service the new properties.

'Probably just another rumour,' I said to Viv.

Within days of Tina's news, a meeting had been

arranged with the *alcaldesa* (mayor) Maite Rodriguez Gomez. She was leader of the Partido Popular group who ran the council by virtue of having four councillors against three from the opposition group, the Democratic Coalition of Parcent. I quite liked Maite; I had met her many times in the village or at the post office and she always seemed pleasant and welcoming to the many expats who had taken up residence in the village. Short and stocky, well-dressed and generally perfectly coiffured, she had a beguiling smile which she readily diffused to anyone who lingered long enough to make her acquaintance. She appeared committed to helping foreigners integrate with the local Spanish community in Parcent. Various events had been organised including musical concerts, history talks and dancing classes to which everyone in the village was invited. We were also invited to the *pensionistas* free Christmas lunch. The town hall also organised Spanish classes for expats and Maite had personally presented Viv and me, and the rest of the class, with official certificates at the end of our beginners' course.

But it was at this hurriedly arranged meeting I suddenly saw a different side to our smiley happy mayor as we embarked on a sequence of events that would see us lock horns, not just with Maite, but with the Partido Popular and the powers-that-be in the Generalitat de Valencia together with one of Valencia's richest and most powerful property developers.

The meeting in the mayor's office at the town hall was hastily arranged and attended by just a few local residents, the mayor and the council's *Tecnico* (technical officer). We were lucky to have the services of Hans, a Dutch neighbour who spoke fluent Spanish and who was able to interpret for us. Despite the *alcaldesa's* usual cheerful demeanour, there was tension in the air as we demanded to know what was going on.

There was, Maite explained, a draft plan for some more houses, but it was just that – an outline proposal, nothing more, so there was no need to be concerned. In no mood to be fobbed off with platitudes, we asked to see the plans. Suddenly the *Tecnico* sprang into action, lifting a vast stack of papers and placing them on the mayor's desk. They looked like a very comprehensive set of documents – about six expensively bound booklets and a whole sheaf of folded plans. Anything but a "draft plan" I thought. One of the large plans was spread out across the desk and we were left to make sense of it. There, in glorious technicolour, was a detailed plan of our area complete with roads and plot layouts with annotations to denote the scale and type of houses to be constructed. The road through Tina's garden was there for all to see, together with an extended road network to serve the new houses – some four hundred in all – comprising villas and blocks of apartments up to four storeys high.

The questions came thick and fast: Who was the developer? Was the council in favour of this idea? Why hadn't we been informed before now? Would we be consulted? Could we object? With hindsight, I realised we were extraordinarily naïve, for we had imagined this was happening in England, under English planning laws, and our rights would be safeguarded by a democratic process. But this was Spain and, as we were soon to discover, Spain's idea of democracy differs substantially from that of Britain (or anywhere else in the civilised world). A Spaniard later explained to me that unlike Britain, where we had had the benefit of over four hundred years to fine-tune our democratic processes, Spain's democracy was still in its infancy having emerged, somewhat haphazardly, from the demise of General Franco in 1975 – as if that were an excuse.

With Hans interpreting, we gradually came to the nitty-gritty of what was proposed as the *Tecnico* calmly explained that the area in which we lived was zoned as "urbanisable" in an old plan – the *Normas Subsidiarias* – dating back to the 1980's. This meant that any developer could, in theory, propose new construction and that there was a presumption in favour because of the existence of this old plan. Then came the most devastating news. The development was being put forward under LRAU, the dreaded Valencian "land grab" law (*Ley Regulador de Actividad Urbanistica*).

Everyone had read about LRAU, indeed an organisation had been set up in the Valencia region to protest and campaign against its iniquities – *Abusos Urbanisticos No* (AUN). Like most people, I guess, I dismissed most of the horror stories associated with this law. They seemed so outrageous, so impossibly extreme, I assumed that people caught up in such problems had probably flouted the law and built illegally in the first place. I was in for a rude awakening.

Our small development had been in existence for

almost twenty years, so how could it be swallowed up in a much larger plan being put forward under LRAU? Blithely the *Tecnico* explained. Ours was an unfinished urbanisation; it had never been formally "adopted" by the town hall because the roads, sewers and street lighting had never been completed by the original developer. The new plan would complete the urbanisation and all the necessary infrastructure, for the existing properties as well as for the new houses. Almost smiling, he continued. Under LRAU, as we would all benefit from the new development and as *the value of our properties would be enhanced*, we would all have to contribute to the developer's costs in installing the infrastructure for the whole of the scheme.

The next question was obvious. How much?

I recall he rubbed his chin and shuffled from one foot to the other, all the while avoiding eye contact. Finally he spoke. 'Well, it is difficult to be precise. The terrain here is quite difficult with steep gradients, so the sewer works in particular will be complicated, but on average similar schemes have cost around seventy-five euros per square metre.'

I swear he smiled smugly as he said this.

'Per square metre?' What did he mean?

'It's quite simple,' he said. 'Any landowner within the development will be required to pay seventy-five euros for every square metre of their plot, including the existing property owners.'

My mind was working overtime. My plot, I knew, was one thousand four hundred square metres. Multiplied by the *Tecnico's* estimate I was facing a bill in excess of one hundred thousand euros – along with all my neighbours.

'This is outrageous,' we protested. 'None of us has this kind of money. What happens if we cannot pay?'

'Then the developer can put a charge on your property or you will have to forfeit some of your land.'

Now I realised why it was called "the land grab law."

To this point Maite had remained in the background. Now all eyes turned to her. 'We have all bought our properties in good faith. How can you allow this to happen?'

Her answer, delivered with a characteristically nonchalant shrug of the shoulders, was simple. '*Es la ley.*' (It's the law.)

At this point Maite left the room leaving us all dumbstruck. As we, too, left the town hall, Hans said to me, 'Mark, we need a lawyer, a good one, and quick.'

As I trudged back alone through the streets of Parcent where I had previously felt so welcome and happy, my mindset suddenly changed. It was obvious the plans we had just seen had been in preparation for a long time. It was impossible to believe they had just emerged out of the blue; the town hall must have been colluding with the promoter for months.

Later this led me to say to a friend that all the while our precious Maite was smiling to our faces, she was actually stabbing us in the back. My friend was quick to point out that it would be impossible to do the two things simultaneously – but he did not know our dear *alcaldesa* as I did.

So there it was; the earthquake that sent shock waves through Avalon and threatened to turn our mythical paradise into a modern day Gehenna.

Chapter Two

So there we were, threatened with financial ruin and the prospect of our sleepy little development being engulfed by a massive housing estate. But, 'There's no point in being despondent,' I said to Viv who was already surfing the web pages advertising property for sale in the UK. 'It may never happen, and in the meantime, there's no reason why we can't get on with our lives and enjoy all that Spain has to offer. Besides, until this business is sorted out, our house is virtually worthless.' At this point the lid of the laptop slammed shut and Viv muttered something from Laurel and Hardy about "a fine mess."

Floating on the pool one day, reflecting optimistically on all the things we had yet to discover about Spain and all the places we had yet to visit, I had just about managed to convince myself that life wasn't so bad after all and that this development business was just a bad dream. With that single caveat, life was free and easy, enjoyable and stress free. Suddenly Viv, who had been busy applying factor-fifty sun cream to Jessie's nose ('dogs get sunburn as well, you know, and they are susceptible to skin cancer') commented casually, 'The pool needs topping up.'

Glancing sideways from my advantageous position, prostrate on the lilo, I realised she was right. The water level was one or two tiles lower than normal. 'It's just evaporation,' I said, paddling toward the steps. 'I'll put the hosepipe on for a while.'

I whiled away another hour or so, drifting aimlessly on the lilo, listening to the faint buzz of the water meter as it clocked up another few euros, until the normal level was achieved. 'It's worth it,' I said to myself. 'I just couldn't survive in Spain without a pool – in the summer at least.' There were times when even I doubted the veracity of my own self-conviction on this subject. A villa on the Costa Blanca with a pretty garden and its own private pool – this was everybody's dream, wasn't it? What I had failed to realise was the amount of effort and expense involved in maintaining this luxury. Constant cleaning to remove dead leaves and insects – even the occasional drowned rat – meant I spent more time, winter and summer, brushing, scrubbing and vacuuming than I did actually swimming. Then there were the expensive chemicals – bucketfuls of chlorine, PH regulator and something called flocculant required to congeal the finest dust particles which eluded the sand filter.

Next morning the water level appeared to have slipped down again. I couldn't be sure so I topped it up once more and this time made a mark on the tiles to indicate the line of the meniscus. The following day my worst suspicions were confirmed. The level had fallen again, by about an inch – much more than could be accounted for by the effects of evaporation. The pool was leaking and I needed help.

Determined by now to rely on Spanish expertise whenever possible, I called in Sylvestre from a local company that specialised in building and maintaining pools. He arrived promptly as promised at five in the afternoon at the conclusion of his siesta. Clean shaven and well groomed with short cropped black hair, he looked very proficient in a smart blue boiler suit and carrying a canvas holdall that obviously held the tools of the trade when it came to diagnosing sick swimming pools.

Sylvestre began by testing the water (why, I was not sure) adding drops of chemicals to two phials of pool water only to confirm what I already knew – the chlorine and PH levels were perfect. Next he inspected the pump room, only to confirm something else I already knew – there was no sign of a leak in the pipe work. Finally, he wandered slowly around the perimeter of the pool inspecting the terrace and surrounding garden to confirm again something I had already sussed out – no sign of dampness.

'What do you think?' I asked apprehensively.

'*No sé*,' he started ('I don't know'). 'There's nothing obvious, no damp patches, no leaks in the pump house, no sign of a crack in the pool walls.' He scratched his chin.

'So what's the solution?' I asked.

'In my experience these things sometimes resolve themselves. It's probably best to leave it a while and see what happens.'

With that, he departed saying, 'Give it a couple of days, a week or so perhaps, and give me a call.'

His answer was less than convincing and the hope that he was right lasted until the next morning, by which time another inch of water had leaked away. Reluctantly, I decided to call on a bit of help closer to home.

The boom in the expat population corresponded

with a burgeoning of British pool "experts" offering their services in pool maintenance and repair. Only later did the thought occur to me that swimming pools were not exactly commonplace in the UK, and I had never heard of a City and Guilds in pool care.

Steve, Ted and Dave each came and went, offering little more than bafflement and conjecture. Steve suggested digging up the terrace to inspect the buried pipes. (Out of the question.) Ted proffered the view that we should look for a crack in the side walls which could easily be filled. (My underwater inspection with snorkel and goggles had already ruled this out.) Dave, the most optimistic of the bunch, offered the opinion, 'It's probably the lights. I've experienced this before.' His solution was to allow the water to fall below the level of the two inset pool lights and see if it stopped there. (I did and it didn't.)

Who needs a pool anyway? I thought. If all else fails we can fill it in and plant some more lemon trees.

I was still calculating the volume of earth required to fill a pool eight metres long by four metres wide with an average depth of two metres, when a letter arrived folded and wedged in the wrought iron gates at the front of the house. The same letter had been circulated to all of the fifty or so families who would be affected by the development proposals which I had managed to put to the back of my mind. We had been summoned to a gathering of local residents to discuss the development issues.

This first attempt at organisation did not go well. The chosen venue was the grand *Cooperativa* with its small bar and great hall. Whilst the bar was generally busy, the hall itself was usually empty, save for a few townsfolk playing cards or dominoes. No one had thought to ask permission to use the hall and, as it gradually filled with residents who quickly started rearranging tables and chairs, I began to notice a few bemused glances from some of the locals using the bar. When someone switched off the wall-mounted television (I swear no one was watching it anyway) the bemusement turned to indignation. Great, I thought, our first meeting and we have managed to offend some of the locals whose support we may ultimately need. Discussions commenced and for a while I feared an outbreak of hostility.

We were rescued by the fortuitous presence of one of the opposition councillors, Pablo. He politely explained that the *Cooperativa* was, strictly speaking, a members-only institute and though the public were generally allowed in "under sufferance" (and to boost bar sales) we could not just commandeer the hall for our meeting. I was sure there were others present who were seeking to have us all ejected. In the end, a compromise was reached and we were allowed to transfer to a small snooker room upstairs. (I call it a snooker room as it was centred by a snooker table of sorts, though I could never fathom it out since it had no pockets.)

With standing room only and packed like sardines, our meeting got underway. It was shambolic. All kinds of rumours were flying around; some people expressed utter disbelief and others suggested the whole thing was nothing but scaremongering. A few people wanted to do nothing, just wait and see how things panned out. Others were ready to storm the town hall there and then.

It was left to a Dutchman from a nearby village to bring some semblance of order and reality to the proceeding. I never did find out how he came to be at our meeting, but he had suffered similar problems where he lived and his message was loud and clear. The plans and the potential consequences for local residents were very real. We needed to discard all thoughts of how such issues would be handled in our home countries and understand that, in Spain, things were dealt with very differently. For a start, if the plans were given the go-ahead by the town hall, then the developer would assume all the legal powers of a public authority – to charge for infrastructure, to sequester land and do pretty much what they damned well liked. We could always try to negotiate with the developer, but we had to do that from a position of strength, and that meant getting organised and fighting every step of the way. He finished by saying unequivocally that we would be fighting corruption and skulduggery on an unimaginable level; things would get nasty, acrimonious, even downright aggressive. We had no alternative but to take the fight to the town hall and the developers themselves, otherwise we would all be shafted. He turned out to be ominously prophetic.

It's a bit like the chicken and the egg – which came first? Was it paella or was it the paellera in which the dish is cooked? The consensus of opinion is that it was the paellera, said to have come from the Old French word *paelle* which in turn derives from the Latin term *patella* – a large flat dish on which offerings were made to the Gods. Armed with my brand new steel paellera and with an "authentic" recipe taken from a book on Spanish cuisine, I embarked on my first attempt at traditional paella Valenciana. Since this was the region from which the dish originated, I felt sure I could recreate something more or less authentic. I had all the ingredients – chicken, pork, prawns, mussels, olive oil, red peppers, beans, stock, some *very expensive* saffron, and of course rice. But my first attempt was bedevilled with problems and turned out to be an utter disaster. For a start the paellera I had bought, some twenty four inches in diameter, was at least large enough to cater for eight people so the ingredients I had to hand (enough for Viv and me) barely covered the surface area. Added to that, I was cooking on the kitchen hob and the largest flame was too small to produce an even heat in the giant pan, meaning that the ingredients burnt in the middle, but barely cooked around the outside. But the principal problem arose because I used normal long-grain rice. This, I was to learn, was akin to sacrilege and produced a soggy mush that resembled a savoury version of rice pudding. Not an auspicious start.

Lessons. (1) Buy a paellera of a suitable size for the number of people to be catered for. (2) Buy a gas ring (to be attached to a canister of butane gas) with one, two or even three concentric burners so that the flames are at least the same diameter as the pan. (3) Use proper paella rice – preferably the best quality *arroz bomba* which is grown in the Valencia region. Back to the drawing board.

From my personal experience I can fairly say that the Spanish are a wonderful race of people; friendly, warm hearted, generous and generally cheerful, even in the face of adversity. As with any general rule there are always a few exceptions (as I was to discover) but my abiding impression of the vast majority of Spanish people remains constant.

Our old friend Pepito whose small plot of land we traversed daily on our walks with Jessie, continued to bemoan the state of the rural economy in these parts as he had done almost every day for the two years we had known him. But he did so with an air of resignation that never detracted from his generally cheerful demeanour. Now in his late seventies and suffering the onset of glaucoma, he still chugged daily to his plot on an ancient *mula mecánica* which looked to be at least as old as him. He was always willing to enlighten us with his wisdom when it came to planting and harvesting his meagre crops.

Seeds should always be sown on a full moon, he told us, as the gravitational pull of the moon would help the seeds germinate and pull the seedlings from the ground. A regular dusting of sulphur powder would ward off insects and deter mildew. Too much water is bad for the plants as they become lazy and their root systems fail to develop. The roots must be made to work and then they can survive and thrive with minimal support.

'It's the same with people,' he said philosophically. 'If they are handed everything on a plate, they become shiftless and then when hard times come they lack the nous to get by.'

I did wonder if he might be having a dig at me in

my state of early retirement in which work of any kind was more of a hobby than a means to an end. But, as if to demonstrate that he bore no ill will, we rarely left his plot without a handful of whatever crop was in season.

I secretly admired his tranquil, uncomplicated way of life; labouring on his land just a short drive from his house in the village and growing the food to put on his table. His needs were basic and his diet was simple. I spoke to him one day about the wedding of a distant cousin he had attended the previous weekend at a smart hotel in Gandia. It was a lavish affair by all accounts and he appeared rather dismissive of the extravagance.

'The food must have been good,' I remarked.

His nose crinkled and his bushy eyebrows drooped beneath a deep furrowed frown. 'It was terrible,' he snapped. 'Far too fancy and much too rich.'

'What did they serve?' I asked, puzzled at his obvious distaste.

'Smoked salmon, and pâté made from ducks' livers or some such thing. The main course was fillet steak smothered in some kind of cheesy sauce. And the pudding was a pile of pastry balls filled with cream and drizzled with sweet sticky chocolate.'

'Profiteroles,' I said, as I began to salivate.

'Crap,' he announced, poking out his tongue and feigning to vomit.

'What would you have liked to eat?' I asked, showing my incredulity.

'Rice,' he said with an air of indignation.

'Rice?' I replied, still surprised.

'Yes, rice,' he affirmed. '*Arroz brut, arroz a banda, arroz negro, arroz de marisco*, or better still, my favourite, paella.'

'Paella?' My interest was suddenly aroused. 'You have a recipe for paella,' I asked.

'You'll have to speak with my wife.'

As I left, still none the wiser in my quest for a pukka paella, he called me back.

'Here take these,' he said, thrusting a bundle of shrivelled runner beans into my hand. The pods were yellow, turning brown and had a dry paper-like feel, almost transparent. Inside each pod I could see several light brown beans mottled with specks of purple. The beans were hard and dry and I could only imagine they were seeds for planting next year. I said as much to Pepito at which point his face creased with a benign smile.

'They're for paella.'

Clearly I had a lot to learn.

Within a few weeks of this encounter we noticed Pepito and a couple of helpers digging around the perimeter of his plot and inserting fence posts. I did wonder if this might be in response to our regular "trespass" on his land as it provided a convenient shortcut between one of the mountain roads and the *camino* that led to our house. I spoke to him about this one day and he explained, somewhat apologetically, that people had been stealing some of his crops and in one case a whole row of tomatoes had been ripped up by vandals. Perhaps sensing my expression of disappointment, he was at pains to explain.

'It's not your fault,' he said, 'but I have no choice.

There will be a gate at each end and I can give you a key if you like.'

I thanked him for the offer, but declined. Somehow it just wouldn't have been the same to be given a kind of privileged access to his land. It saddened me to think that throughout his life Pepito had been able to leave his land open and unguarded and I wondered, then, what forces had brought about this shift, and what Pepito must think of the changing times in which we lived. In the months that followed we saw less and less of Pepito on his allotment and the following spring we noticed that the whole plot was untended and overrun with weeds.

I bumped into Pepito one day working inside a small lock-up garage in the centre of the village not far from the post office. An electrically powered machine, rather like a garden shredder, was grinding away at the back, taking whole almonds from a hopper, spitting out the hulls into an ever-growing pile and depositing the hard nuts into a sack attached to the side. Pepito himself sat at a workbench taking almonds, one at a time, and bashing them with a mallet on a wooden block to crack the hard shells and extract the kernels which he placed in a polythene bag. It was slow, laborious work that required interminable patience for very little reward. I called out to him and enquired after his health, but when I spoke he did not seem to recognise me. Only after standing and walking from the gloom of the garage into the brighter light of the street did he realise who I was as he squinted through cloudy eyes. A smile crossed his face and he shook my hand enthusiastically. He invited me inside and beckoned me to sit on a stool at the side of his bench.

Seemingly glad of the company, he told me that glaucoma had forced him to abandon his allotment. 'When you can't tell an apple from a tomato, it's time to give up,' he said. 'Besides I am no longer fit to drive the *mula mecánica*. My sons pick the almonds and olives when they have the time, but they don't have the time or the patience to grow vegetables.'

I said I was sorry to hear that, but he replied resignedly. '*Los años no pasan en balde*,' he said, which roughly translated means – the years take their toll.

'That's true,' I replied, trying to think of something equally apposite. '*El tiempo y la marea no esperan a nadie*,' I said, wondering whether the time and tide adage would strike a chord in Spanish.

Pepito responded with an understanding smile. 'Make the best of your youth,' he told me, leaving me to ponder on how to feel youthful in my retirement.

One of our favourite bars in the Valley was Bar Varetes in the village of Lliber. It was run by Manolo and his wife Lina, and to us it became known as Lina's bar. It was nothing to write home about, just a small village bar with six or seven tables and a fruit machine that competed noisily with the wall-mounted television which seemed *de rigueur* for any Spanish bar. Its best feature by far was the small outdoor eating area that nestled in the corner of the small village square. This location was marred only by the presence of a public telephone kiosk that made it possible to listen in to conversations whilst enjoying a coffee or a snack.

We spent many enjoyable evenings and lunchtimes in this square, usually with our friends Pat and Les who seemed to share our appreciation of the informality of the place and Lina's genial hospitality. Our normal fare was tapas which varied daily according to what was available. Lina would just recite a list and we would choose six or seven plates. Liver, sliced pork, calamari, fried fish, chicken wings, meatballs, mushrooms, mussels, artichokes, peppers, aubergines were the most usual offerings. Whatever we ordered, the dishes arrived one at a time, freshly cooked by Lina, along with bread and alioli and (at Viv's insistence) a plate of *patatas fritas*.

There is something about this kind of informal eating – everyone picking from shared plates of food – that engenders a relaxed mood and makes for good conversation. Viv and Pat found that ability, only ever encountered amongst the female of the species, to talk about feelings and emotions, whilst Les and I stuck rigidly to our male stereotypes and talked about politics, sport and economics. As a foursome we spent many enjoyable hours at Lina's bar, sharing conversation and laughter and what the Irish would call "Craic" (crack). This generally meant that no subject was off limits and gentle (or not so gentle) teasing was given and taken in good heart.

For quite a while we assumed that tapas was all that Lina had to offer until one day, in a casual aside, Lina asked if we would like something else.

'What else do you have on the menu?' we asked, to which Lina replied, 'What would you like? Just tell me and I will cook it.'

We never expected haute cuisine, but when Lina

mentioned entrecote steak, chips and char-grilled vegetables (with fried egg) we just had to give it a try. 'Just let me know the day before and I will buy everything in fresh,' Lina said. And excellent it was – with a simple salad starter and a modest pudding (usually from the chill cabinet) this was undoubtedly the best steak and chips ever experienced in a small village bar, in the shade of a false pepper tree, with beer mats propping up the table legs to counter the gentle slope in the village square. It became a regular event and we lingered at Lina's bar on many a balmy summer evening watching village life and putting the world to rights. When, eventually, we asked for the bill, Lina would just return and tell us the total amount due. We never did see a bill, so it is hard to attach a price to the steak and chips, save to say that we were always surprised at how cheap it was. When we paid, Lina would always offer us a complimentary glass of sweet *mistela* or a herb liqueur called *orujo* that was bright, luminous green in colour and definitely warmed the cockles, sending us on our way feeling gleeful and replete.

And then one day I spotted it – a table set for six with a large round wicker mat placed in the centre. When the diners gathered, it wasn't long before Lina brought out a large, steaming paella and they all tucked in.

'I didn't know you did paella,' I said to Lina. To which she replied, 'I've told you, if you order in advance, you can have anything you want.'

It just had to be done....

A week or so later we occupied our usual table by the telephone kiosk in anticipation of the big event.

Les just happened to mention that our meal was part of the research for my latest book – "*En búsqueda de la paella perfecta.*" Lina's eyes lit up. '*Es aquí. Tu lo ha encontrado,*' she said. (It's here. You have found it.)

Whether it was this incentive or just Lina's standard fare, I'm not sure, but the paella was enormous and very tasty too. By now it was becoming clear that there was no such thing as a standard paella and, like so many home-spun recipes, they each varied, probably according to family tradition. Lina's version contained all the familiar ingredients – rice, chicken, rabbit, runner beans, butter beans and garlic with a liberal topping of char-grilled red pepper and prawns and garnished with wedges of lemon. Everything was cooked to perfection with a perfect *socarrat* – the prized burnt caramelised layer of rice that has to be scraped away from the bottom of the paellera. But there was one added component which I had not encountered before – chickpeas. They didn't add much to the flavour but, in modern chefs' parlance, they added another texture – a bit of extra crunch.

As we left, having paid another bargain-priced bill, Lina called out, 'I hope you will give me a good write-up.'

'I'll do better than that,' I replied. 'I'll put you on the front cover.'

Jessie was reaching an age where an early morning walk and a short afternoon stroll gave her enough exercise in between meal times and enabled her to relax and snooze through most of the rest of the day.

I sometimes wished I could have said the same, but there always seemed to be something to do or somewhere new to go.

It was with a degree of surprise that I found Jessie one morning rummaging fervently at the base of the oleander hedge that formed the rear boundary of our plot. She seemed agitated, scratching through fallen leaves and whimpering before squatting on her haunches and focussing her attention on a particular spot just beyond her reach. I decided to investigate, reaching deep beneath the hedge to disturb a pile of rotting leaves. Ouch! Something pricked my finger, drawing blood. Further investigation revealed the culprit to be a baby hedgehog curled up into a tight defensive ball. I should probably have left it alone, but Jessie's frantic barking suggested this was not an option. So I gently lifted it out of its hiding place and placed it on the edge of the patio. Jessie's curiosity was not assuaged as she pawed at the tiny ball, rolling it around. It was only when she tried to nuzzle and sniff the infant hedgehog that she admitted defeat and made a strategic retreat, hunkering down about a yard away to keep it under close observation. It became a battle of wills as both Jessie and the hedgehog remained motionless for the next two hours in a kind of stubborn standoff. So still was the hedgehog, that if it wasn't for a vaguely discernible pulsation of the prickly ball, it would have been easy to believe the poor thing had died of fright.

Finally the prickle-ball began to unfurl. A tiny head was first to emerge with blinking eyes that reminded me hedgehogs are essentially nocturnal. Then four short, clawed feet were revealed and it made its first tentative steps. To our amazement (watching the whole episode from the comfort of two sun beds on the terrace) the hedgehog moved slowly in Jessie's direction until they were literally nose to nose. Perhaps wiser after the first encounter, Jessie seemed unperturbed by the visitor and was content simply to watch as it scuttled over the patio.

'It'll be hungry,' Viv said. 'We should feed it.'

'But what do hedgehogs eat?' I asked, fearing we were on the verge of acquiring a new pet.

The first saucerful of bread dipped in milk went down very well, though my research on the internet led me to discover that this was very bad for hedgehogs, causing diarrhoea. Cat food was the recommended diet, so I was despatched to the shops with Viv's words ringing in my ears, 'And don't buy any cheap stuff, those little foil pouches would probably be best, but not the ones containing fish. I don't think hedgehogs eat fish.'

I surmised there was a certain logic to that, since a hedgehog in its natural surroundings was unlikely to encounter the salmon, trout or prawns that formed a part of the ingredients of gourmet cat food.

'Have you seen the price of luxury cat food?' were the words I dared not utter when I returned.

The Spanish word for hedgehog, I discovered, is *erizo*.

'Then that's what we'll call him,' Viv decided.

'How do you know it's a male?' I asked innocently.

'Same as with any other animal,' Viv said.

I couldn't argue with the logic of that, but as Erizo instinctively curled up into a defensive ball when handled, I settled for accepting that he was a he, wondering if he happened to be a she we should be calling her Eriza.

I was not sure hedgehogs made good house pets, but I was certain they could not be house trained. So we agreed the best thing to do was to leave him loose in the garden with a nice pile of dry leaves and plenty of cat food and hope that he stuck around.

Two weeks later Erizo was still with us, indeed he had grown from the size of a cricket ball to the size of a... well, not a football, a baseball perhaps. He seemed quite at home in his new surroundings and Jessie's first move each morning was to make a beeline for leaf pile. Despite being nocturnal, he became accustomed to scuttling around the garden during daylight hours, usually with Jessie in close, fascinated attendance. It was as if the two had become friends, quite close one might have said, which was fine until Viv read an article that said hedgehogs are frequently infested with fleas. Her first thought, naturally, was that Jessie might become contaminated. Now the notion of keeping a flea-ridden pest in the garden did not seem such a good idea, to Viv at least.

I just knew what was coming next and I wasn't wrong.

'Is there any of that insecticidal dog shampoo left?' she asked.

Much as the thought of giving a hedgehog a full shampoo and set amused me, I had my answer prepared.

'Hedgehog fleas are specific to hedgehogs,' I said. 'So there's no fear of cross-contamination.'

'Don't be ridiculous,' Viv replied. 'Fleas are fleas. How can a flea tell the difference between a hedgehog and a dog?'

'It's true,' I stated. 'I read it on the internet this morning. Did you know there are more than a million different species of insects adapted to every kind of environment? So I guess it's not inconceivable that there's one that likes to live exclusively on hedgehogs.' The marvels of the animal kingdom never cease to amaze.

As things turned out, the situation resolved itself when Jessie, on one of her early morning patrols, came up with a blank. Erizo had moved on to pastures new and we never saw him/her again.

'Did you know?' I said to Viv a few days later. 'Romany gypsies used to eat hedgehogs. Apparently they would wrap them in clay and bake them in the embers of a fire. When baked hard they would crack the clay and pull away the spines to reveal the flesh.'

Viv seemed uninterested in this revelation, so I resisted the temptation to wonder out loud whether they killed the poor hedgehog first. And then it occurred to me... Erizo was an easy word to remember because it sounded like chorizo the famous spicy Spanish sausage.

'Here, you don't think Erizo ended up in a paella do you?'

I had to duck to avoid the shoe that was flying in my direction.

Chapter Three

'We need a lawyer, a good one, and quick.' With those words still echoing in our ears, a group of residents started making enquiries about legal representatives who might help us confront the town hall and the developers. As in the rest of the world I guess, there was any number of lawyers (*abogados*) willing to take on the work. The problem was finding someone with knowledge of Spanish urbanistic law and with an interest in more than just the fat fees they could charge. Then there was the perennial problem of the language barrier. Several of our group had a passable understanding of Spanish, but everyday conversation is one thing, understanding the practices and processes of the Spanish legal system was something entirely different.

We talked to a great many people and took advice which ranged from 'a nice bloke, but totally useless' to 'don't go near him, he's a complete shyster.' Finally we received a positive recommendation. Within days, a representative group of residents was gathered in the austere offices of a firm of lawyers situated on Denia's grand, tree-lined boulevard, the Marques de Campo. Our contact lawyer, an associate of a prominent law practice based in Valencia, was James, an Englishman who had lived in Spain all his life and qualified in law at Valencia University. He was a phlegmatic character who seemed slightly more comfortable speaking in Spanish (his native tongue) than in English. He looked very lawyerly in his smart suit and tie as he positioned himself defensively behind an expansive mahogany desk flanked by shelves stacked high with leather-bound law books. He must have wondered about the casually dressed bunch who sat before him who, if I say so myself, looked as if we had just arrived from the beach.

He listened calmly and quietly as we hit him with a barrage of questions, then followed up with questions of his own to establish our exact legal status. Curiously, he seemed aware already of the existence of the plans for development in Parcent. Finally, he announced his willingness to represent us in protecting our interests and professed his familiarity with cases similar to ours. He was confident that through due process we could, at the very least, stall the plans and protect our interests, if not thwart the plans completely. To do this would involve tracking every stage of the planning process, presenting objections at every opportunity and even taking our case to the courts.

All this sounded very promising, but there was one obvious question. How much?

From my previous experience with lawyers in England, I had expected the 'how long is a piece of string' speech – hourly fees, expenses, disbursements and the like. James surprised us all by stating that the normal practice (in Spain) was to fix a fee to be paid 'up-front' which would cover us for all costs up to reaching a 'satisfactory conclusion.' Leaving aside the question of what constituted a 'satisfactory conclusion,' we were all still anxious to learn the exact amount.

'Around twenty thousand euros,' was his answer.

Expensive as this may sound, we were lucky (if that is the right word) that we were a group of around fifty families and the cost, shared between us, seemed manageable – so long as everyone agreed to pay their share. As things turned out, there were a couple of recalcitrant owners. One couple took an ostrich-like stance, believing it would never happen, but hoped we would keep them 'in the loop' (freeloaders). Another couple said they could not afford their share of five hundred euros as they were saving up for central heating. (I resisted the temptation to point out that they may not have a house worth heating if the plans went ahead).

Although reassured after our meeting with James, my natural scepticism would not allow me to countenance paying the whole of his fee up front. He may have been more Spanish than English, and this may have been the way things were usually done in Spain, but I had to point out that he was dealing with a group of mainly English residents and this was not the way we expected to do business, even if we were in desperate need of his services. So we negotiated a system of staged payments based on work undertaken and everyone seemed relatively happy with this.

On James's advice we quickly organised ourselves into a formal Residents Association complete with an official constitution translated into Spanish and registered with the relevant authorities. All we needed to do now was appoint an Executive Committee, Secretary, Treasurer and Chairman. There were ready candidates for most of these posts, but for the post of Chairman we clearly needed someone experienced in dealing with local councillors; someone adept at organising and running meetings; someone used to dealing with lawyers; someone who was skilled in assimilating information and writing reports. At the Association's first formal meeting the chairman was elected unopposed.

'You could have said no,' was Viv's first reaction. 'We've come all this way to Spain to get away from the stress of work and now you've landed yourself with another job and unpaid at that. Are you so bored with your new life that you just had to get back in the old routine? I expect you'll be disappearing to meetings at all hours, hogging the computer and wriggling your way through sleepless nights, just like before. We might just as well have stayed at home. Why couldn't someone else be chairman?'

'Well actually,' I said, 'I've not been elected chairman. You see that term does not readily translate into Spanish and the word does not exist in our official constitution.'

'What the hell are you jabbering on about?'

'I've been elected *El Presidente*.'

'Well Mr *El Presidente*, just don't expect my help in running your little bloody empire.'

In a way Viv had a point. Neither of us imagined when we left dear old England that we would find ourselves doing battle with the powers-that-be, not just to stop the developers, but to safeguard our (and everyone else's) financial future. What I could not tell Viv at the time was that I was racked with guilt because, through my impatience and impetuosity, I had landed us in Casa Emelia in the first place. I had secretly vowed that I would move heaven and earth to get us out of the mess I had created, if only for my own self esteem – even if there were to be a few fractious moments along the way.

It was at that point I heard some plates crash in the kitchen.

The water level in the pool was still falling and I was nowhere nearer to finding a solution. On my travels through Benissa one day, I happened to spot a small corner shop displaying pool equipment and advertising its services in pool maintenance and repair. There were many such outlets dotted around our locality, but bearing in mind the ambivalent advice I had received so far, I had steered clear. However, what attracted my attention to this particular establishment was the fact that the shop signs were in German. Now, I know that the German's have a reputation for lacking a certain sense of humour, but they also have a reputation for efficiency and hard work and this, I decided, was just what I needed if I were ever to float on my lilo again.

The next day, Wolfgang and his son Ernst arrived at Casa Emelia for a tour of inspection and they quickly sprang into action. The first thing to do, Wolfgang said, was to pressure-test all the pipe work. To do this they had to completely drain the pool. Much as I despaired at the thought of thousands of gallons of expensive water going to waste, within minutes the pump was running and a rivulet of chlorinated water was flowing through the hedge and down the hill in the road outside our house.

'Just keep an eye on it and make sure you turn off

the pump when the pool is empty,' Wolfgang said. 'It'll take an hour or two. We'll be back after lunch.'

Within half an hour of their departure I had answered calls from two of my neighbours who had seen the flood outside the house and asked if we had a leaking water pipe. I explained what was happening and received one response I could have done without.

'Seems a bit extreme to me,' one neighbour said. 'I'm sure there's a way to test the pressure without draining the pool.'

I decided not to enquire further, convinced that this piece of information was about as useless as all the previous advice I had received. I was content to rely on the German experts, I told myself, resisting the temptation to imagine Wolfgang and Ernst stuffing themselves at lunch with bratwurst and sauerkraut, washed down no doubt with a stein or two of pilsner.

It must have been a good lunch as the pair did not return until four o'clock, seemingly sober and ready for action. Ernst dropped to the deep end of the now empty pool and clamped a tight rubber bung in the water outlet and then repeated this process in the skimmer outlet. Meanwhile, Wolfgang attached a gauge to the pipe work in the pool house and pressurised the whole system.

'That's all we can do for now,' Wolfgang announced. 'We just have to see if the pressure remains constant and then we'll know if there's a leak in the pipes. We'll be back in the morning to take another look.'

I was tempted to sit in the pool house overnight and monitor the gauge, but settled instead for a sleepless night wondering if a leak in the pipes was a good thing or not.

Within weeks of our first meeting with James the lawyer, he informed us that a public notice had been posted in the official Valencian Bulletin inviting bidders to submit proposals for the development of what was now referred to as Sector Repla, the area surrounding our houses. And within weeks of that notice we heard that a second plan had materialised, submitted by a notorious speculator renowned for his shady land deals and dubious methods. Montessori's plan would have involved the construction of six hundred houses together with the requisite infrastructure.

To this point none of the affected residents had received any kind of official notification from the town hall. But then a strange thing happened. The man behind the first plan made contact and invited us to a meeting. He had obviously heard of the *Asociación de Vecinos de Sector Repla*, as we were officially titled, and wanted to enlist our support. We saw no harm in opening up a channel of communication, even though our suspicions were aroused when we heard he was the brother of Isandro, one of the Partido Popular councillors – the councillor with responsibility for *Urbanismo*!

The meeting was scheduled for mid-afternoon in the shade of our pergola. When he arrived, Ramón Puig was strangely familiar with Casa Emelia, which was not so strange when he explained that he had built the place along with most of the other houses now embroiled in his latest plan. He was sweetness and light, explaining his willingness to discuss any aspect of his plan. But it turned out that the main purpose of his contact was to encourage us to object to the alternative proposals submitted by the shady Señor Montessori. He did his utmost to denigrate Montessori, pointing out that the plan he had submitted was basically flawed because Montessori had stated in the documents that he was the owner of all the land in his plan – something that was patently untrue, not least because Puig said that *he* owned most of it. He even went so far as to present us with a document of objection which we could sign and register with the town hall.

Two things emerged from this meeting. The first was that Puig was obviously aware of the formation of our Association and saw benefits in getting us on-side with his plans. The second was that he was more concerned with protecting his own plan than making any real concessions. In short, we did not trust the man.

It wasn't long before Montessori himself was in contact, and though some neighbours felt we should steer clear of this rogue, the consensus was that we should at least listen to him, if only to be fair to both parties.

A more obsequious man would be hard to imagine. Dressed in a sharp, shiny suit and tie and accompanied by an attractive secretary who was there to interpret, he regaled us with every kind of promise, even going so far as to suggest we could join in his project if only we supported his plans and opposed those submitted by Puig. We gained the impression that if we wanted marble pavements and gold plated lamp posts anything was possible. He assured us of his high reputation as a developer and allowed his secretary to tell us what an honest and trustworthy man he was. He barely blinked when I asked him why it was that the documents supporting his plan claimed, erroneously, that he owned all the land. He simply shrugged and suggested this was just a trifling oversight that could easily be rectified.

One thing emerged from this meeting. We did not trust Señor Montessori one inch further than we could have thrown him and his servile secretary. (Much later we heard that a warrant had been issued for the arrest of Montessori following the illegal redevelopment an office block in Javea. He was rumoured to have fled to Romania to start up another property scam).

Having met our two potential protagonists we were quietly satisfied that we had made an impression. They were both clearly aware of the existence of our Association and evidently saw us, and our lawyer, as a threat. If nothing else we had established a position of strength. But our confidence was to be short lived. As the deadline approached for the submission of plans for Parcent, we heard rumours that a third plan was about to emerge. With just hours to go before close of play, I was stationed in the town hall with a couple of neighbours. With just minutes to go before the town hall was due to close, an executive four-by-four pulled up outside. The boot opened and three young men began to unload pile upon pile of papers, plans and folders, depositing them on the reception desk and waiting whilst each one was officially stamped in and receipted. Worse news was to come. This third plan had been submitted by a subsidiary of the Barrera Group, one of the biggest property developers in Spain and run by one of Valencia's richest and most influential entrepreneurs. The plan covered the whole of Sector Repla and made provision for *two thousand* new properties, mainly apartments, covering more than a million square metres of Parcent's most precious and beautiful countryside and swallowing up our small urbanisation into what would have become a giant urban blot on the landscape. One strange aspect of the plan was the inclusion of what was referred to as the *Avenida Diagonal* – a four lane, tree-lined dual carriageway which curiously began at the eastern end of Sector Repla pointing towards Jalon and ended at the western boundary pointing towards Benichembla. In its scale and ambition the *Avenida Diagonal* rivalled its namesake in central Barcelona, except that it was the road to (and from) nowhere. Small wonder it sparked rumours of Señor Barrera's lofty ambitions for the rest of our precious valley. If we were worried before, we were petrified now, and all the odds seemed to be stacked against us. We also heard that plans had been submitted (at the invitation of the town hall) for the development of two other areas in Parcent which, together, would have brought the total of new houses up to three thousand five hundred. The combined effect would have been to increase the population of Parcent from around one thousand to almost ten thousand and turn our remote country village into a small metropolis.

I couldn't help thinking at this stage about the election manifesto issued by Maite and the Partido

Popular just a year or so earlier. True, there was mention of the need to develop plans for the future of Parcent, but I also remembered clearly the promises of "transparency and full consultation." Politics in Spain were, it seemed, much the same as anywhere else – parties made promises to get elected and then ploughed on regardless with what they really wanted to do in the first place. Even so, this was deceit on a massive scale, and we were not alone in thinking this way.

Talking to local Spanish friends, I found it difficult to find anyone who supported what was being planned for their village. Naively, I asked one Spanish friend why this was happening if no one, except the controlling councillors, wanted it. After looking around furtively, he winked and tapped his back pocket. 'Money, that's what it's all about,' he said, adding, 'and not for the village.' Though he said this, it was without anger or outrage and it was then I began to realise that a level of impropriety was tolerated, even expected, in local officialdom. Even so, it seemed to me that this was abuse of power on a colossal scale.

Chapter Four

The German pool experts, Wolfgang and Ernst, returned as promised and promptly announced that the pressure in the pipes had remained constant overnight.

'*Alles in ordnung*,' Wolfgang stated.

Perhaps I should have been pleased, but the way the pair of them rubbed chins and scratched heads led me to believe this was bad news. After dismantling their equipment and stowing it in the van, they both descended the pool steps and gave the tiles a closer inspection, focussing their attention on the far side wall. There was something of a "eureka" moment and Ernst called me down to join them.

'There is your problem,' Wolfgang announced, pointing at the side wall.

I studied it carefully, but could see nothing amiss.

'What am I looking at?' I asked.

He ran his hand over an area of tiles which looked fine to me. 'You see this brown staining in the grout.'

I looked more closely and could see an area of about one square metre where the white grout had indeed stained brown.

'Look, there's more here… and here,' Ernst said, shuffling along the wall toward the deep end.

As I looked, I could clearly see several more areas of brown stained grout.

'What is it?' I asked.

'Rost,' Wolfgang said.

'Rost? What is rost?'

'How do you say it? Wolfgang questioned. 'When iron goes brown.'

'Rust you mean?'

'That's it, rust. You have rust in your pool.'

This was bizarre, I thought. How could I have a rusty pool? Wolfgang explained. When a pool is built, the excavated hole is first lined with an intricate framework of heavy steel reinforcement rods. These form a foundation onto which a special kind of concrete (called Gunnite) is sprayed to create the base and walls before the tiles are applied. Normally this Gunnite forms a durable, waterproof layer and the tiles are mere decoration. However, it sometimes happens that the Gunnite perishes over time. This allows water to leak through the walls causing the steel mesh to rust and the stains leach back. Hence the brown staining to the grout.

'But the pool is just fifteen years old,' I explained. 'Can this happen in that time?'

Wolfgang explained that it can and does happen. The Gunnite might have been wrongly mixed in the first place or applied too thinly or... 'It could be that olive tree.' He pointed to the ancient olive tree just three metres away from the side wall of the pool which had provided Viv and me with very welcome shade during many afternoon siestas.

'If that's the problem, what's the solution?' I asked, fearing the worst.

Ernst was sent out to the van and returned with a bundle of brochures, samples of kind of rubberised material and a selection of new tiles. It was left to Wolfgang to explain.

First they had to pressure-hose the whole pool to remove dirt and loose grout. Then they would apply three coats of a special resin material to form a completely sealed "rubberised" lining for the whole pool. Finally they would re-tile and re-grout the whole pool. It would, they assured me, be as good as new... if not better.

'And the cost?'

After the two of them had measured the length, breadth and depth of the pool, they joined me at the table in the naya and Wolfgang began tapping busily on his pocket calculator.

'Depending on your choice of tiles, it will cost around seven thousand euros.

I blanched. This was definitely not in our carefully constructed ten year budget plan. And since we were already facing the threat of bankruptcy, courtesy of the avaricious property speculators, I began to feel the onset of a very painful headache. It wasn't just the cost that bothered me; how was I going to explain all this to Viv?

'Is there an alternative?' I asked.

'Not if you want to use the pool again,' Wolfgang announced.

We parted amicably and I promised to think about it and get back to them. Wolfgang kindly left the brochures and samples with me and I got the impression he knew I would be back in touch.

'How much?' Viv exclaimed. 'That's a hell of a dent in our budget just so that you can float on your lilo and contemplate your own navel. I hope you like beans on toast.'

To her credit, she could have mentioned how I

had rushed into coming to Spain, and how I had talked her into buying Casa Emelia before she had even seen the place. But she left it at that and allowed me to grapple with my own conscience and wallow in my own sense of guilt.

'There is an option,' I said, having already thought this out.

'But I thought the Germans said there was no alternative.'

'I could do all the work myself. It would be much cheaper.'

'Have you seen the size of the pool? Have you ever done any tiling before?'

'I tiled the bathroom at Heath Lodge, don't you remember?'

'You can't be serious.'

Indeed I was. It couldn't be that difficult... Could it?

Our small urbanisation was occupied almost exclusively by retired expats – mainly British, German and Dutch. I sometimes thought it was like living in one of those retirement villages with alarm buttons to summon help and a hot-line to the local ambulance station. There was, however, one exception to this stereotype, a young British couple, Stuart and Angela, who had come to Spain to work – Stuart as a chef, Angela as a... well, actually I don't think she worked at all. We got to know them quite well with Viv taking particular interest in the small ginger and white cat they had taken on as a stray. Lucy occasionally wandered into our garden, which wasn't a problem except... whenever Lucy appeared,

Jessie would make a beeline for her and Lucy would high tail it in the direction of the front gate. It wasn't that Jessie was aggressive, indeed quite the opposite. Jessie had lived with a cat for some years back in England with very few problems. Admittedly, Mac, as we called him, had established a well-trodden high-level route from the cat flap, onto the kitchen work surface, across the table, along the dresser and out into the relative safety of hall. Even so, there were a few direct confrontations from which Jessie would always back down.

When Stuart and Angela suddenly announced they were returning to the UK, Viv's first question (naturally) was, 'What's happening to Lucy?'

'We can't take her back to the UK,' Stuart said, 'so she will have to be re-homed.'

It was a no-brainer, at least for Viv.

'But the cat is plainly terrified of Jessie,' I said in a vain attempt to ward off the inevitable.

'They'll be fine,' Viv said with confidence.

Within days I was cutting a hole in the external door to the dining room to accommodate a cat flap. And within a few days more, aided by the judicious placement of a bowl of cat food, Lucy had mastered her private ingress and egress. And within a few days of that, Jessie had learnt to recognise the sound of the cat flap and shoot to the dining room to greet her new friend, prompting Lucy to beat a speedy retreat.

'I told you it wouldn't work,' I said. To which Viv replied, 'Just be patient.'

A month later we had acquired a child gate to wedge between the hall and the dining room so there was at least one room Lucy could enter in relative safety. It didn't seem to matter to Viv that every time I needed something from the dining room I had to dismantle and re-erect the child gate. Even this arrangement was not good enough.

'There's no heating in the dining room. Lucy needs somewhere warmer to sleep,' Viv announced.

And so a second child gate was installed across the entrance to the spare bedroom. The only problem now, for Lucy, was the five metre length of corridor between the dining room and her sleeping quarters. Which wasn't a problem at all as Lucy quickly mastered the art of peering through the gate in the dining room to check that the coast was clear, and then sprinting to the bedroom before Jessie had even noticed. It didn't seem to matter to Viv that our house was turning into an obstacle course – Lucy was happy.

'It won't be for ever,' Viv said. 'Things will soon settle down and they'll become friends.'

Famous last words. Two years later, and in spite of many determined attempts by Viv to engender friendship and tolerance, the obstacle course was still firmly in place.

Sadly (he says without a hint of sarcasm) Lucy contracted cancer and died a little while later. Offers were invited for a couple of child gates that were surplus to requirements.

As a group of foreign residents, we felt rather isolated from the village and the thought crossed my mind that in opposing the town hall and the developers we might be at odds with at least some of the Spanish population. After all, they had elected their councillors and perhaps there was support for more development and the jobs that might come with it. My concerns were not assuaged by the few local people I had spoken to who seemed at best indifferent to the plans.

Luckily not everyone in Parcent felt the same way. We began to hear of stirrings in the local population as opposition to the plans emerged. Soon we learned of the formation of *Veins de Parcent* (roughly translated as Neighbours of Parcent). Articles opposing the plans began to emerge in the local press and banners declaring, *"Salvem Parcent"* (Save Parcent) began to appear on village balconies. Someone had organised the production of "before and after" images of the three development plans showing the true horror of what the future might hold.

For our Association it was good to know that we were not alone and many expats joined with *Veins de Parcent* in their protests and to raise money for the fight ahead. We seemed to have a common objective in opposing the town hall, though I did not realise at the time that our Association was viewed with some suspicion. The problem was that we had a financial motive for fighting the town hall, whereas Veins had more principled objections to the ruination of their village. Nevertheless, we were invited to join local Spaniards who were raising a petition against the plan. At least a third of Parcent's adult population were expats so I guessed they needed our support. In the next few weeks every house in the village was visited and jointly we managed to gather the signatures of some five hundred and eighty-five residents – well over half the adult population of the village. As *El Presidente* of the Association, I was invited to present the petition at the town hall with a Spanish neighbour, Juan, representing *Veins de Parcent*. We met as arranged on the steps of the town hall and I was surprised to be surrounded by a phalanx of reporters and cameramen. Before I realised what was happening, we were at the town hall reception desk as flashes popped to record the moment the petition was officially presented and stamped in.

Ten minutes later, I found myself in the sitting room at the house of Juan's grandmother, just a short distance from the town hall, hosting an impromptu press conference. The questions came thick and fast and though my Spanish was improving, I was relieved that Juan, a teacher, was able to interpret. I was expecting a hostile grilling along the lines of – why did a bunch of foreigners think they had the right to interfere in local politics? To my surprise (or more likely because of Juan's careful selection) the reporters were more interested in the theme of people-power taking on the vested interests of politicians and property developers. And Juan, ever the diplomat, stressed the uniqueness of our campaign with local people and foreign residents working together in a common cause.

The next morning, Juan and I featured prominently in several local and even some national newspapers. All the articles followed a common theme – a majority of Parcent's population had signed a petition rejecting the idea of such massive development and calling on the town hall to abandon their plans. Surely, I thought, if there was any vestige of democracy in Parcent, the town hall would have to listen.

Then summer arrived and, as in most of Spain, everything went quiet as the fiesta season began.

All the villages in the valley organised their own fiestas throughout July and August. They usually lasted a week or more and as one finished another would start. Although they each had their own unique events, they also had their common features – a candle light procession when the statue of the village's patron saint is taken from the church and paraded through the streets; several nights of very loud music continuing until the early hours; a communal dinner in the streets; children's parties; a firework display of Olympic proportions; and bulls careering through the streets.

It is virtually impossible for anyone who is not of Spanish extraction to understand the true significance of fiesta. Although religion is always at the heart of fiesta, it has developed a tradition of fun and entertainment together with a spirit of friendliness and tolerance which has become part of Spanish heritage. Someone once explained to me that in bygone days people could not afford to travel on holidays and so the holidays were brought to them. That would certainly explain why whole villages stop work for a week and why participation is virtually compulsory. However, fiesta is much more than just a week's abstinence from work. It is more a celebration of community spirit; an opportunity for disparate families to reunite; an affirmation of religious faith; and above all, a celebration of life itself. It is perhaps for this reason that fiesta is observed as enthusiastically as ever even if it has, to some degree, moved with the times. And it appears to me that there is a certain amount of village pride, if not rivalry, involved as each village tries to out-do the others in the extravagance and exuberance of their individual celebrations.

Since the *raison d'être* for fiesta is an enigma to most expats in Spain, the majority of us (me included at times) fail to embrace its true spirit. One example of this misunderstanding is evidenced annually in the letters pages of the local English language press. The most common source of indignation is the loud rock music that booms through the night air from midnight to dawn on three or four consecutive nights. 'Don't they realise it's hot in summer and we have to keep the windows open?' And, 'Why must they let off fireworks at seven in the morning to wake everybody up?'

But that's the whole point of fiesta – you are not supposed to sleep; young or old, you are supposed to make the most of the week-long party – there's time to catch up on sleep when it's over.

Another frequent source of criticism is the extravagance of the firework displays that would put many a small city to shame. I suppose this criticism is sparked (excuse the pun) by the fact that residents are expected contribute to the costs of fiesta in what many foreigners see as a "fiesta tax." It's a voluntary contribution, of course, but when faced with a group of young *Festeros* knocking on the door, most people pay up, albeit reluctantly, with typically British self-restraint. I guess it's hard for some people to watch their contribution of thirty or forty euros per family literally going up in smoke, but then again, a fiesta (or almost any celebration in Spain) simply would not be the same with fireworks – and there's no point in doing things by halves, is there?

Another source of indignation, especially to us animal loving Brits, is the bulls. I've witnessed a few rather tawdry spectacles of bulls being herded from transporters to be stampeded through streets and squares, prodded and cajoled along the way, some with flaming torches attached to their horns. Whatever I may think, I have come to realise that when it comes to bulls, there is something deeply embedded in the Spanish psyche – a kind of admiration balanced with a desire for domination.

There are signs that traditional bullfighting is on the wane. It has been banned in some regions, though I think this has more to do with falling attendances and perhaps boredom with the bloody spectacle of ritual slaughter when the result is almost always Matadors six – Bulls nil. Even so, no village fiesta in these parts would be complete without the running of the bulls.

A couple of years ago a notice appeared on the doors of a local town hall on the first day of the fiesta. It stated that there would be no bulls this year because the *Festeros* had insufficient funds. There was an outcry amongst traditionalists and two days later it was announced that the bulls had been reinstated – paid for by the town hall.

I made a point of not venturing an opinion on the subject, though I did mention it in passing to a young Spanish friend. His retort was short and concise.

'Well, at least we don't chase foxes to their death with a pack of hounds and a troop of red-coated horsemen.' End of subject.

One event that occurs quite regularly in some village fiestas is the giant paella, indeed there are companies that specialise in this type of outdoor catering event. In my pursuit of the perfect paella, this was something I could not miss. So when one such event was announced in a nearby village I set off early, keen to learn.

I knew I was in the right place when I spotted a large white van parked at the side of the square with a giant paella dish strapped vertically to the side. It resembled an enormous satellite dish about three metres in diameter with two sets of handles welded on opposite sides. I was keen to take notes of the recipe, but it was quite some time before anything edible emerged from the van.

The first items to be unloaded were twenty or so breeze blocks which the two male attendants quickly arranged into a circle of six columns each about two feet tall. I was impressed when the men used a long plank and a spirit level to adjust the height of the columns to counter the effect of gentle incline in the surface of the square. Clearly they had encountered this problem before. Next to emerge from the van was a stack of firewood comprising kindling and what I perceived to be old staves from wooden barrels. Within minutes, and aided by a dousing of paraffin, a substantial bonfire was ablaze on the cobbled surface at the centre of the columns. When, eventually, the flames abated, the men kicked around the embers to spread them evenly around the circle. The giant paellera was untied from the side of the van and placed on the columns. At last it was time to cook.

For anyone interested I have set out below the recipe instructions. The quantities stated are sufficient for around one hundred people so you will have to adjust them for smaller gatherings.

- Pour ten litres of olive into the paellera and heat until just smoking.
- Add six bucketfuls of chicken roughly hacked into pieces, followed by an equal quantity of mangled rabbit, and the same of roughly chopped belly pork.
- Using a giant wooden spoon (about six feet long) stir the meat and cook until nicely browned.
- Next pour in a sackful of short grained paella rice – about fifteen kilos should be enough – and mix well with the cooked meat.
- Add about fifty litres of stock (chicken I think) preferably hot. (You may find a separate brazier useful for this purpose.)
- Next add ten kilos of cut green beans and four catering tins of butter beans along with ten whole garlic bulbs.
- Stir everything again then reduce the heat to a simmer (rake the embers or add some more wood, depending on how well the fire is burning) and then leave everything to cook WITHOUT STIRRING until the rice has absorbed all the stock. You will know when the paella is cooked when the stock stops bubbling and the whole dish

begins to sizzle.
- Finally, just before serving, sprinkle the surface of the paella with about three kilos of roughly chopped canned roasted red peppers.

At last it was time to eat. People formed orderly queues and the two attendants scooped generous portions of paella onto paper plates and issued everyone with a plastic fork. The fork was fine for shovelling up the rice and vegetables, but as most of the meat was on the bone, it was about as useful as a pierced soup spoon. So everyone resorted to fingers, which resulted in a crowd of people with greasy fingers searching for napkins that were not provided. The verdict: well, for mass catering it wasn't bad – a little bland, I thought, under seasoned (as chefs would say) and very greasy. The search for the perfect recipe went on.

At the end of the event everything was packed away, including a dozen or so bin-liners bulging with bones, paper plates and plastic forks. The breeze block columns were dismantled, the remains of the fire were doused and swept away (leaving a patch of scorched cobble stones) and finally, the giant paellera was strapped back on the side of the van. Which left one question: How on earth do you wash a three metre paella pan?

Chapter Five

Wolfgang was surprised, if not incredulous, when I appeared in his shop to announce that I was planning to undertake the pool repairs myself. After his initial shock and several minutes of pleading – did I know what I was taking on? – he finally agreed to supply me with all the materials and a great deal of practical advice. There was just one proviso – if I did the work myself, he could not guarantee it.

'But you are sure this plastic material will do the job and stop the leaks?' I asked.

'Applied properly, yes,' he replied. 'Don't skimp though. It will need a minimum of three thick coats and then everything should be fine.'

'But this stuff is designed for the purpose?' I asked.

'Well, no. Actually it's more often used to waterproof underground car parks and such things, but it will work fine on your swimming pool. If you don't believe me, contact the manufacturers in Germany.'

I did just that, emailing a company called Schomburg in Detmold, Central Germany. My German is rubbish so I was not too hopeful. Within twenty-four hours, Bernhard replied with a four page specification for the product *Aquafin-1K-Flex* which detailed the product's tensile adhesive strength, tear strength, crack bridging capability and pressure resistance – and much, much more – all in English.

Bernhard also assured me that though the product was designed for other uses, it would certainly fix my pool leaks.

A few days later I took delivery of thirty, very expensive, twenty kilo bags of Aquafin-1K-Flex, which Wolfgang unloaded from his van with a final plea. 'Are you absolutely sure you want to do this?'

I answered in the affirmative, trying to look confident if not blasé.

'Then take my advice,' Wolfgang said. 'Follow the manufacturer's instructions to the letter; mix it well and don't mix too much at once. This stuff sets quite quickly and it is very, very sticky.'

Then next day I was up at the crack of dawn to make an early start. The pool had already been jet-washed and was ready for the first coat. I poured half a bag of the dry powder into one of those large rubber buckets the Spanish use for everything. Next I added the stated amount of cold water and began to mix with a trowel. Ten minutes later I was still mixing the sticky grey slurry, trying to eliminate lumps. My wrist was aching and I was convinced that more water was needed. I checked the instructions, only to confirm the quantities were correct, and finally stepped down into the pool starting at deep end. Two hours later and using the biggest paintbrush I could find, I had finally exhausted the first batch. My arm was throbbing with the effort of spreading the gungy grey splodge which had the consistency and adherence of a thick (very thick) Yorkshire pudding batter. I stood back to admire my work and calculated that I had covered approximately five square metres. My mental arithmetic told me that at this rate I would need about sixteen more batches at two hours each. That meant thirty-two hours, plus mixing time. This was going to be one hell of a job. And then I remembered – it needs three coats! Two things were clear: I needed a better way of mixing the powder and water; and I needed a bigger brush.

Well, I'd started so I was going to finish. I bought an attachment for my electric drill which resembled a giant Yorkshire pudding batter mixer. Though my drill could be heard whining under the strain, it did the job of whisking the gunge to stiff peaks. I also bought a large, soft bristled sweeping brush with which to apply the stuff. It had two advantages: I could grab it with both hands thereby reducing the strain on my arms and shoulders; and coverage was much quicker. I pressed on, covering all the walls and then set about the floor, working from the deep end to avoid painting myself into a corner. With breaks for rest and regular upper body massages from Viv, the first coat was finished – and in just three days! Just two more coats to go.

Then it rained. I can personally testify that *Aquafin-1K-Flex* is fully waterproof for now we had a large puddle at the bottom of the pool. Since said material must (according to the instructions) be applied to a surface which is perfectly dry, I had to find a way to get rid of the water. Those big rubber buckets are indeed very useful. With Viv's help we formed a chain gang (if you can call two links a chain) with me scooping up the water and lifting the bucket up to Viv to dispose of the water.

Luckily the weather stayed dry and progress continued, though I must admit I awoke each morning with less and less enthusiasm for the task.

'I just have to go to the market in Jalon this morning,' I said to Viv. 'We're running low on carrots.' (Or potatoes or mushrooms or whatever I could think of). Anything to avoid doing battle with another bucket load of Aquafin. I swear I was having nightmares about the stuff as I waded waist deep in a sea of grey gunge that, like a quicksand, grew ever deeper as I struggled to escape. 'Help me Wolfgang, I'm going to drown.'

'You need to take a break,' Viv said. 'At this rate *El Presidente* will be in no fit state to do battle with the powers-that-be and then we might find the pool has been repossessed.'

Spurred on by these encouraging sentiments, the third and final coat was applied two weeks later and we now had a magnificent pool with a beautiful shiny grey plastic lining. All it needed now was tiles. How difficult could that be?

Whilst I laboured, the rest of the population seemed to be in permanent fiesta mode. The council in Parcent had gone into recess without responding to our petition and all was quiet on the development front, or so it seemed. When I finally caught up with our lawyer James, it was clear he had been hard at work. He had spent his summer preparing detailed objections against the plans for Sector Repla which challenged almost every aspect of what was being proposed, including the legal status of plan in itself.

These objections had an effect and before I could make progress on tiling the pool we received another approach from Ramón Puig wanting to discuss his proposals. In fact he became a regular visitor to Casa Emelia to hold talks with the Association's Executive Committee and our lawyer. Ramón expressed his willingness to discuss any aspect of his plan. If we didn't like the road layout, he would change it; if some of the new houses were too close to existing property he would move them; if we wanted to form a kind of consortium of owners with him, he would welcome it. Then he delivered his *pièce de résistance.* If we went along with his plan we wouldn't have to pay a penny in infrastructure charges and no one would have to forfeit land. Victory, some might have assumed, and so did we as we continued to meet with Puig and later his consultant architect to explore this proposition. But then a curious thing happened. It was only a shifty glance in answer to a seemingly innocent remark, but it became apparent that Puig was not acting for himself – he had thrown his lot in with the Barrera Group. His *pièce de résistance* came with a *quid pro quo* – the acceptance of two thousand houses on our doorstep.

Even so, the offer was on the table – no infrastructure charges. Was this not the raison d'être of our Association – to protect ourselves from potential financial ruin? We had to put it to a vote. With Viv supplying the coffee and unstinting encouragement, I hugged the computer and worked late into the nights trying to put together a balanced report which outlined the intricacies of the offer that had been made and set out objectively the pros and cons of accepting or rejecting the offer that was on the table.

Rumours of this proposition quickly spread

amongst our Spanish neighbours and the hierarchy of *Veins de Parcent*. This was what they had feared all along – a group of foreigners, concerned more about their pockets than the future of the village, would surely sell out. They could well be right, I thought, as I knew that for some members of the Association, the fear of financial ruin had caused sleepless nights.

As we approached the crucial meeting, I was contacted by several Spanish neighbours asking what was likely to happen in the vote. Their apprehension was obvious and understandable – if we "sold out" it could sound the death knell for opposition to Barrera's plans.

There was a long and well-informed debate and I made a point of not expressing a personal opinion. However, when the vote came, I was happy to be amongst the first to raise my hand. The offer from Puig, on behalf of the Barrera Group, was rejected virtually unanimously. I was so proud of the members since we had demonstrated our solidarity with the majority of our Spanish neighbours and shown that we were not simply concerned about our own financial interests. On hearing the news, our lawyer, James, emailed me to say, 'Congratulations. A very brave decision.' It was then I realised what a seminal moment this was, and from that point on I sensed that our relationship with our Spanish neighbours changed, but in some cases for the worse.

Back to the pool and those tiles. One spin-off from our spat with the town hall was that I had made the acquaintance of a young Swiss neighbour who had taken on the refurbishment of a magnificent house owned by his aging parents. The house was not strictly in the area affected by the development plans, but it was close enough for him to be concerned. Approaching forty years of age, Jean-David was one of those people who was annoyingly fluent in several languages including French, Italian, German and Spanish. Even more annoyingly, he was comfortably adept at just about anything he turned his hand to – including the construction of a swimming pool at his parents' house. On a visit to Casa Emelia he expressed interest (or more likely puzzlement) in our shiny grey plastic pool. He had never seen anything like it. When I explained that it was just a matter of applying the tiles, he asked me over to his house to see the pool he had recently installed. Some pool – it was in the shape of a huge figure-eight with an arched wooden bridge spanning the narrowest part and a built-in Jacuzzi adjacent to the poolside decking shaded by a Greco-Roman style pergola. He had planned and designed the whole thing himself and constructed it with a little help from a few local labourers.

'Do you like the tiles?' he asked.

They were mid blue colour, azure you might say, similar to the sky on a clear day and not dissimilar to the colour I had in mind for our own pool.

'Very nice,' I replied.

'Then you might be interested in what I have in my garage.'

The double garage door was raised to reveal a huge stack of boxed tiles covering almost a quarter of the floor area.

'I over-ordered,' Jean-David said.

Not such a clever-clogs after all, I thought.

'They can't be returned so you can have them if you want.'

By my quick calculations there were enough tiles to cover almost half our pool and Jean-David told me the name of the supplier so I could order the rest. And if I wanted, I could put them through his trade account and obtain a discount on the retail price.

What a lovely man.

'Who is doing the tiling?' he asked.

When I told him of my DIY plans, he tapped me gently on the shoulder. 'Mark, even I wouldn't attempt that. It's a job for the experts. When you order the extra tiles you need to ask for *los Basques que ponen azulejos*. (The Basques who install tiles).

So it was that ten days later two Basque brothers arrived at Casa Emelia early one morning to tackle the stack of boxed tiles and the small mountain of bagged adhesive powder. Experts they certainly were. By mid-afternoon, we had a sparkling new pool exactly the colour of the sky on a clear day.

'We'll be back in the morning to do the grouting,' they said. 'It will only take an hour or so.'

They were true to their word and as I stood back to marvel at our brand new pool which was (almost) all my own work, Viv joined me on the terrace.

'What do you think?' I said, trying to disguise my pride and suppress a self-satisfied smile.

'I would have preferred a darker blue,' Viv said.

So, was it worth it? The answer has to be yes, since we saved over three thousand euros on the original estimate, in part due to the generosity of Jean-David donating his surplus tiles. He insisted, however, that we were doing him a favour as he had to dispose of them somehow. The only cost to us was a fine meal which we were happy to provide to express our gratitude.

After a week or so to allow the new tiles and grouting to set, it was time to fill the pool. Strictly speaking, so I was told, we were not allowed to fill the pool from the tap since drinking water is a precious and expensive commodity. To discourage profligacy, drinking water is metered and the price per unit increases exponentially the more you use. To have filled the pool from our tap would definitely have put us in the red zone. Instead we should have bought water to be delivered by tanker, but the price including transport was just as expensive. So we cheated. As luck would have it, our Dutch neighbour was away for the summer and therefore not using any water at all. I connected a long hosepipe to his outdoor tap and left it running in the pool for over twenty four hours on the understanding that I would pay the whole of his water bill for that quarter. Job done, or so I thought. When the pool was full with "drinking" water it was so pink and cloudy it was impossible to see the bottom at the deep end. And to think we had been drinking this stuff. The solution was to add something called flocculant which attracts particles of dirt and forms a kind of gel that sinks to the bottom from where it can be vacuumed to waste. Perhaps a water tanker would have been a better idea.

As summer turned to autumn it emerged that, far from listening to public opinion or taking note of our lawyer's objections, the mayor and the other ruling councillors had been holding secret meetings with the developers. They were, it seemed, determined to press on regardless. I had to wonder what drove them on in the face of objections, threats of legal action and overwhelming opposition from a majority of the local electorate. (Readers will have to reach their own conclusions.)

A small glimmer of hope appeared on the horizon when we heard from our lawyer that, in response to criticism in the European Parliament, the *Generalitat de Valencia* was about to abolish LRAU and replace it with a new and "fairer" law called LUV – *Ley Urbanistica de Valencia*. James's initial assessment was that this new law would not prohibit the kind of development proposed, but it would require greater scrutiny and there would be more stringent requirements for consultation and improved rights for people who were directly affected. The only problem was that LUV would not come into effect until the following February.

As the dark nights of winter lingered beyond Christmas, outrage suddenly burst forth. A meeting of the council had been arranged for the end of January where the plans were to be discussed. Protests were planned and *Veins de Parcent* organised a march through the streets. Though I didn't condone it, graffiti began to appear – *Construcción si, Destrucción no* (and far worse). Some scallywags even went so far as to over-paint all the signposts to Parcent with "*Marbella*" – a reference to the fact that the mayor of the Andalucian resort had recently been imprisoned for corruption. I couldn't help but smile.

As the date of the planned council meeting drew

near, temperatures rose, metaphorically, if not literally. On a rainy afternoon, just a few days before the council meeting, I was surprised to find Ramón Puig on my doorstep. He looked bedraggled and forlorn and wanted to talk. My Spanish had improved considerably in the previous few months, but it was impossible for me to understand Ramón's frantic gabbling. Luckily my Swiss friend Jean-David was at home and willing to come to my rescue. We put another log on the fire and Viv brought fresh coffee and brandy (not the good stuff, obviously) as we waited for Jean-David to arrive.

What happened next was remarkable. Poor old Ramón poured his heart out. He never wanted to side with Barrera, but what could he do? This man was far too wealthy and powerful to resist. In return for his coalescence, he had been appointed as an associate of Barrera's company and was authorised to negotiate on their behalf. If only we would reconsider his earlier proposition we could avoid all the controversy and end the acrimony and disharmony in the village.

I was unmoved and said so.

Then he changed tack. 'You don't realise, Mark (we were on first name terms by this stage) what it's like in the village at the moment. My house has been daubed with graffiti and my car has been vandalised. Worse still, yesterday someone spat at my mother in the street. She's eighty-six you know. If you would just reconsider, we could put a stop to all this.'

It was clear from the dark rings beneath his eyes that he had been suffering sleepless nights and for a fleeting moment I felt sorry for him. But then I thought about the way he had systematically deceived us through meeting after meeting only to find he was acting for Barrera all along.

'I'm sorry to hear of your problems,' I said. 'I don't condone graffiti or vandalism and I certainly don't approve of the abuse your mother has suffered. But it seems to me that you can easily put a stop to all this. Just persuade your brother to vote against the plans at Monday's meeting.'

A big turnout was expected for Monday's night's meeting; it was, after all, the most important in Parcent's history. The opposition group called for the meeting to be moved to another venue as the small council chamber had seating for just fifty people with perhaps another forty standing in the wings. The request was refused.

That afternoon I called in at the town hall hoping to speak to the Secretary to the Council. I had met Javier on a few occasions and, though he was keen to remain impartial as his role demanded, I felt he was someone we could trust. My instinct was right. In the privacy of his office he disclosed that some months earlier he had sought a kind of "Counsels' Opinion" from high ranking legal officials in Valencia. The purpose was to test the proposition, often put forward by the *alcaldesa*, that the council had no alternative but to approve the plans because the land was zoned urbanisable in that old *Normas Subsidiarias* plan. He showed me a copy of the opinion he had received. It was twenty pages long and in Spanish, but he pointed me to the summary at the end and translated. Clear as day, it said there was considerable doubt about the validity of the *Normas Subsidiarias* as a legal basis for the approval of development on such a large scale.

It went on to state unequivocally that, if they so wished, the council could reject all the plans that had been submitted. It seemed like good news, but I could tell from Javier's demeanour that all was not as it seemed. He had passed a copy of the opinion to all the councillors, but the Partido Popular had rejected it as simply advice and not legally binding. They planned to plough ahead regardless.

Whilst with Javier, I asked him about the position of Isandro, the brother of Ramón Puig, who was councillor for *urbanismo,* and in particular whether, legally, he was entitled to vote on his brother's plan. The law book on his desk was already flagged at the relevant page and he translated the pertinent section. *"No councillor may vote on any matter in which he/she or any of his/her blood relatives have a substantial interest."* It seemed clear to me, but then Javier identified a problem; Ramón's plan had been withdrawn.

'But what of the Barrera plan and Ramón's position as an associate, and the fact that he still owns a substantial amount of land in the area?' I asked.

'You would need to check that out for yourself,' he said.

I did just that. Within hours our lawyer had searched the online *Registro Mercantil* and there it was in black and white. Ramón Puig was listed as an associate of the subsidiary of the Barrera Group in whose name the plan had been submitted. Surely this proved he had a substantial pecuniary interest in the plan and that meant his brother could not vote. With the council balanced at four councillors in favour of the plan and three against, Isandro's disbarment from voting would deny the PP a majority. James emailed me a copy of the *Registro Mercantil* and armed with several more copies I waited in the lobby of the town hall an hour before the meeting was due to start. As each of the councillors arrived (I knew them all by sight) I thrust a copy into their hands and gave them my pre-rehearsed speech in Spanish quoting the exact section of the law and stating that Ramón's brother could not legally vote on the plans. I even gave a copy to Isandro himself. He muttered something about it being history and dropped the paper to the floor.

By the time I entered the council chamber at the top of the stairs, it was already packed to the gunwales. Outside the town hall, a large crowd had already gathered and the local police officer, flanked by two armed officers from the *Policia Nacional*, was refusing admission to anyone else on the grounds of "Health and Safety." The shouting and chanting from outside was clearly audible in the chamber itself. I moved to the balcony on the landing and looked down. It was pouring with rain and below me was a sea of hundreds of umbrellas bobbing up and down in time with the rhythmic chants. Nothing, it seemed, and certainly not a mere torrential downpour, could dampen the fervour of the protestors. But then, suddenly, the crowd fell silent and the strains of dirge-like music emerged from further down the street. I leant over the balcony to see a small musical band heading a funeral cortège with four men carrying a mock coffin inscribed with the words "RIP Parcent". It was followed by a crowd of around a hundred people who swelled the number of protesters to more than two hundred. *Veins de Parcent* had organised the funeral and the coffin which, together with the sea of umbrellas, were soon to become emblematic of the travesty that was about to take place in the council chamber. Flash bulbs popped and TV crews jostled for position; the story was about to go nationwide.

The mayor seemed unmoved as she and the other councillors took their seats on the podium. She smiled at several people in the audience and it was then I realised the room had been packed with Partido Popular supporters. The meeting itself was brief and business-like. Yes there was mention of Isandro and his eligibility to vote. There was a reference to the "counsel's opinion" but when it came to the voting, the Barrera plan for Sector Repla and the two other plans for other parts of the village were perfunctorily approved, each by a majority of four votes to three.

I lingered in the warmth of the town hall chatting with a couple of the opposition councillors. Maite and her cohort were effectively imprisoned in the ground floor offices in fear for their own safety as the crowd, Viv amongst them, lingered despite the deluge for an hour or more. I finally caught up with Viv back at Casa Emelia. After picking my way through the naya, which was strewn with damp clothing, I found her huddled in front of the log fire, dressed in her heavy dressing gown and thick woollen socks, hugging a steaming cup of tea.

'What a disaster,' Viv said.

'I know, it's terrible.'

'Have you seen them?' she said. 'My new boots are ruined.'

It was left to our lawyer to explain what had happened. Ramón Puig had amended the *Registro Mercantil* that afternoon to delete his involvement with the Barrera Group. That didn't mean he was no longer associated with their plan, simply that his name did not appear in the register. As for the counsel's opinion, it had been dismissed as just that – a non-binding opinion. There was some good news though – the Barrera plan had been reduced from two thousand new houses to a mere one thousand five hundred. Great!

Chapter Six

If you put your head above the parapet you expect to get shot at – metaphorically if not literally. And so it was in Parcent. From being an anonymous foreigner in a small Spanish village, I seemed to have gained a degree of notoriety. People I had routinely chatted to in the street suddenly started ignoring me. People in some of the shops where I had previously felt welcome, became brusque bordering on rude. And when I entered a bar, even amongst friends, I noticed small cabals huddling together, pointing and muttering beneath their breath. For some people at least, I was viewed as an interfering interloper, meddling in affairs that were none of my business.

But there are two sides to every story. Fresh fruit and vegetables suddenly appeared at our gate, people I had hardly known before stopped to chat; drinks appeared in front of us when we went for a meal or a snack and we began to receive invitations to informal family gatherings. Not everyone, it seemed, was unappreciative of the stance the Association had taken in opposing the plans.

One family, Juan and Aurora, became particular friends. It was Juan who had accompanied me when we presented the petition to the town hall. Both he and his wife were teachers and lived just a few hundred metres from our house. Cakes and small pastries were Aurora's speciality and we rarely passed their house without being offered something to sample. Juan cultivated a small plot of land near his house and we were often the recipients of the fruits of his labours. Juan and I chatted frequently about all manner of things, but in particular about the state of village politics.

Perhaps it was a quid pro quo for all the gifts, or possibly he sensed I had time on my hands, but one day Juan decided to call in a favour. His seventeen year old son, Juan Junior, was hoping to go to university the following year and a language qualification was a virtual necessity if he were to gain a place. He was studying English but, his father said, he could do with a little help. What could I say? It couldn't be that difficult and it would help my Spanish as well. So we set up a twice weekly one hour lesson at five in the afternoon.

I've never been a teacher and like many other people I presumed it was a cushy job with plenty of holidays. That was until I met Juan Junior. He wasn't an unwilling pupil, though his time keeping could have been better. (I put it down to the fact that he was Spanish). I thought we might be rehearsing verb conjugations or simply extending our vocabulary, but I was wrong. Juan was working to the equivalent of an 'A' Level text book, complete with exercises and tests. I found myself transposing whole texts from direct to indirect speech or being asked to change sentences from the present indicative to the present subjunctive. At school I was never any good at languages, though I did just scrape through 'O' Level English Grammar. But that was forty years ago; now I couldn't recognise the subjunctive form of a verb even though I probably used it every day of my life.

The same can be said of the indicative or the pluperfect or the past perfect continuous. There was only one solution – I had to go back to school myself, spending hours on the computer between lessons with Juan, brushing up on my own English Grammar.

Gradually we made progress, even stumbling through painful explanations of the use of the ubiquitous apostrophe in English. The problem is that this particular punctuation mark just does not exist in Spanish either in the possessive sense (Juan's house) or as a contraction (Juan's not going to school today). We found many "false friends" in our languages – *embarazada*, for example, means pregnant, *carpeta* means folder and *constipado* means to have a bad cold. Small wonder there was plenty of room for confusion.

After ploughing through the exercise book, we would end each lesson with a conversation of sorts, though finding a topic of interest to a seventeen year old was not always easy. Football, I thought, he's bound to be interested in that. A World Cup was approaching and in anticipation of England's usual early exit from the competition, I announced that once they were eliminated I would be changing my allegiance to support Spain. He didn't seem impressed and went on to explain why. He didn't support Spain himself; indeed he did not regard himself as Spanish. He was Valenciano and a supporter of Valencian Independence. He would like, one day, to see Valencia with its own team in the World Cup. When I asked him if that was ever likely to happen, he replied, 'Why not? You have teams from England, Northern Ireland, Scotland and Wales.

Why not a team from Valencia?' There followed some lengthy discussions about the seventeen autonomous regions of Spain – from Asturias to Andalucia – and it wasn't just the Basque Country that would have liked to achieve independence. Juan was scathing about the way the *Generalitat de Valencia* had permitted uncontrolled building along the Costas and encouraged the virtual colonisation of some communities by foreigners. 'Present company excepted,' he was quick to add, though I was not entirely sure he meant it.

After four months, it was time for Juan to sit his English exam and I was almost as anxious as his parents to hear the result. He passed, of course, and secured his place at the University of Valencia. I did ask him if he wanted to continue our lessons, but he politely declined.

As the dust settled on the council's decision to approve the three development plans for Parcent, it was left to our lawyer, James, to explain what had actually taken place. The council had in effect "provisionally" approved three *Programas de Actuación Integrada* (PAIs) under LRAU, just two days before that law was to have been repealed and replaced. It was a devious and underhand manoeuvre and showed the extent to which the council was acting hand-in-glove with the developers. However, James reassured us that all was not lost, in fact this was just the beginning and now, legally speaking, we had something to get our teeth into; something to challenge in the courts. Just as importantly, the "provisional" approval of the PAIs had to be referred to the regional government in Valencia and the whole issue was becoming such a *cause célèbre* that the Generalitat would have to think very carefully before putting themselves in the spotlight.

The problem for the council was that, even under LRAU, a PAI should only be approved if it complied in full with the provisions of the General Plan for the area – and Parcent had no General Plan, only that old *Normas Subsidiarias* plan which was years out of date. It seemed to be a fatal flaw in what the council had done and the ruling councillors were clearly aware of this. A week later the council met again to approve a *concierto previo* (first draft) of a new General Plan and, surprise surprise, all the areas covered by the three PAIs (including that for Sector Repla) were zoned as urbanisable. Even so this was clearly a case of putting the cart before the horse.

Something else became clear at this stage; a political challenge had to be mounted to wrest control of the council from the hands of Maite and her group. The next municipal elections were just over sixteen months away and if the PP could be ousted from the town hall, all might not yet be lost – if we could just stall the plans until then.

In the intervening period both our Association and *Veins de Parcent* remained vigilant and active. *Veins* in particular took their campaign to the streets. Regular demonstrations were organised in Parcent, in Alicante, in Valencia and outside the offices of the Barrera Group. Barely a week went by without TV coverage or newspaper articles. *Veins* also presented a petition to the European Parliament to highlight the iniquities of the Valencian land laws and the extent to which environmentally important land could be ravaged by unscrupulous politicians and rapacious developers, without even so much as an assessment of the impact on the environment or the local community. Representatives of *Veins* visited Brussels more than once to outline their case and a delegation of the Petitions Committee of the European Parliament came to Parcent to be greeted by a sea of umbrellas on a beautiful sunny afternoon.

Complaints were made to the *Sindic de Grueges* (the Valencian Ombudsman) and the *Defensor del Pueblo* (the National Ombudsman). The *Confederación Hidrográfica del Júcar* (the regional water authority) was contacted because there had never been any attempt to assess the availability of water to support such a massive expansion of homes in and around Parcent.

Success after success came the way of *Veins de Parcent* and our Association. The first was a ruling from the *Tribunal Superior de Valencia* in response to a case brought by the Association's lawyers. The judges ruled that the PP controlled council was in breach of proper procedures and had contravened residents' rights in a way that would have left us defenseless against the developer. The ruling went further, however. In a decision which was without precedent in Valencia, the court questioned the "riotous" development of the Valencian Community through the use of PAI's to reclassify millions of square metres of rustic land. It also affirmed that development on this scale was excessive and required a planning process that "weighs the integrated needs of the municipality and its sustainable development."

It suggested that PAI's were not a suitable means to achieve this end and that it required a much more careful and considered process that examined the sustainability of development and its impact on the community.

It was a landmark ruling and became known as "The Doctrine of Parcent." Maite and her cohort immediately lodged an appeal which meant the judgement was effectively suspended.

The *Confederación Hidrográfica del Júcar* issued a report stating that there had been no assessment as to the adequacy of water resources to support the planned developments without which the plans could not proceed. Soon afterwards both the *Sindic de Grueges* and the *Defensor del Pueblo* issued reports calling for the suspension of the plans not least because of the lack of a proper report on water resources.

Now, you might have thought, and we did, that faced with this degree of criticism and adverse judgements, Maite and her colleagues would have backed down. Not a bit of it. They ploughed on regardless seeking to defend their actions at every opportunity. Their principal claim was that the approval of the PAIs was only "provisional" and not therefore subject to the full rigours of the law. But the determination, desperation and sheer deviousness of the *alcaldesa* were yet to be unleashed.

In the breaks between hostilities life went on. There were times when it would have been easy to have become consumed by the problems we were facing, and I have to admit to spending many a sleepless night thinking what else we might do to thwart the powers-that-be in Parcent. All our conversations with friends seemed to be dominated by the topic as people anxiously sought the latest news or perpetuated the latest rumour.

We had to make a determined effort to switch off and resume a normal existence. Our daily walks with Jessie were one way of doing this, not least because they reacquainted us with the wonderful countryside around our home which had attracted us to Parcent in the first place. It was on one such walk on a quiet Sunday morning that we bumped into our old friend Antonio – he who sculptured the carob trees on his plot of land in order to trap wild birds.

He was in a cheerful mood, whistling tunefully as he approached us. With a cartridge belt strung across his chest and a twelve bore shotgun resting on his shoulder, he resembled a Mexican bandit, minus the moustache. Despite his jaunty demeanour it had been a bad morning.

'Only two,' he declared. 'The mist was low and the birds were difficult to flush out.'

'Two what?' Viv asked.

'*Tordos*,' he replied, swinging an arm behind his back to pull forward two dead thrushes dangling from a string attached to his belt.

Viv blanched and uttered a barely disguised 'ugh' of disapproval.

'What's the matter?' Antonio said. 'You don't like *tordos*?'

It's probably just my nature, but as a foreigner in Spain I was reluctant to express disapproval of something as ingrained as hunting was in these parts, so I felt the need to down play Viv's disgust.

'No, no,' I said. 'It's just that in England, thrushes are garden birds. We put food out for them in the winter.'

'And then you shoot them, yes?'

'No. We just like to see them in the garden.'

'Ah, yes,' Antonio responded. 'I forget what a sentimental lot you English are. Have you ever tried *tordos*?'

'Never,' Viv interjected.

'You should do. They're quite a delicacy.'

With that we parted company.

The following Sunday, as dusk fell, there was a knock on the door. It was Antonio looking bedraggled and damp from the drizzle that had persisted for most of the day. I took pity and invited him in, relieved to see that he rested his shotgun against the wall in the naya before entering the house.

'Coffee?' I asked, thinking he might be in need of a warm drink.

'I'd prefer a beer, if you have one.'

I was in the midst of preparing dinner and my usual glass of ale stood on the kitchen counter so I could hardly deny him.

'That's far too much,' he said as I planted a tall tumbler before him, forgetting that customarily Spaniards would drink beer from small wine goblets that, to my mind, barely amounted to a gulp.

He sipped the beer then swung a plastic supermarket bag onto the kitchen work surface.

'A gift for you,' he said.

Viv had joined us in the kitchen and looked on as I opened the bag. Suddenly the air split with a loud ear-piercing shriek as Viv cast her eyes on the contents – a brace of thrushes.

'Get them out of here, now,' she demanded.

His beer unfinished, I ushered Antonio back into the naya.

'I'm sorry if you think us rude, Antonio, but you see we are just not used to having dead birds in our kitchen, especially when they are still warm and fully feathered.'

'It's not a problem, Mark,' Antonio said. 'I can pluck them and clean them if you want.'

'Thanks but no, Antonio,' I said and then, ever the diplomat, I added, 'I wouldn't know how to cook them.'

'That's easy,' Antonio said. 'You cook them in paella.'

This was one recipe I did not want to pursue.

Things were hotting-up in the town hall as Maite the mayor sought to baton down the hatches and nullify all opposition to her plans. Javier, the borough secretary who, to my mind, had acted professionally throughout, was instructed to withdraw from all activity relating to the PAI's and the draft General Plan. The excuse was that the council needed specialist advice on these matters which was beyond Javier's remit. So they appointed another, private, solicitor for this work. Much later we discovered this solicitor was an associate of a legal practice which also advised the Barrera Group. Talk about letting the fox loose in the hen house!

At one stage, as *Veins de Parcent* set up a table at a local fair to gather signatures for the petition to the

European Parliament, the *alcaldesa* sent the local police officer to move them along under threat of arrest. When asked to justify this, Maite said she had issued a personal decree and that her word was law.

It was not the only time she was to demonstrate such tyrannical tendencies. At a public council meeting packed with reporters and cameramen, Maite grew angry at their presence as reporters scribbled and cameras clicked. In a flash of petulance she decided, unilaterally, to have them all ejected. One of the reporters protested and an opposition councillor questioned her ruling. Her answer was symptomatic of her despotic inclinations. 'I am the mayor,' she said. 'This is my town hall and in this place my word is the law.' As clerk to the meeting, Javier, was asked for a legal ruling. His response was remarkable (and brave). 'The last time I looked, Spain was a democracy and the press and public have an absolute right to attend council meetings.'

You should have seen the next day's headlines, accompanied by pictures of a wild-eyed Maite thrusting her arm forward in what might easily have been mistaken for a Falange salute.

When *Veins de Parcent* were invited to Brussels to address the Petitions Committee of the European Parliament, Maite booked a flight for herself and an advisor and attempted to lambaste the committee members without even being invited to speak. Later when the Petitions Committee visited Parcent to meet the public, Maite refused permission for them to use any public building, so we met them in the garden of a private house. Maite did, however, agree to meet members of the Committee privately, at which meeting they were treated to a video presentation by the Barrera Group to show just how nice their development would be.

To counteract the lack of a proper water report, the local *Comunidad de Regantes* (the group responsible for distributing agricultural water for irrigation) were prevailed upon to issue a public statement to the effect that there was plenty of water for all the planned developments in Parcent and the rest of the Jalon valley. No study, no seismographic tests, no measurements – just a bald statement, 'There's plenty of water.'

In another raucous council meeting packed with PP supporters, there was constant barracking when the opposition councillors tried to speak in favour of a motion of censure they had tabled. Refusing to answer any of the points raised in the debate, Maite began a long diatribe which reached a crescendo with the words, 'I believe in a Parcent with a bigger and better school, a Parcent with a new library, a Parcent with more jobs... a *Parcent para todos* (for everyone). At this point I was incredulous and muttered sarcastically under my breath, 'Bah - a *Parcent para todos?*' It was barely a whisper and nothing compared with the previous heckling, but suddenly there was a tumult. All the PP supporters rose as one, pointing at me and shouting, 'Be silent. Show some respect. Throw him out.' Perhaps mindful of the earlier headlines, Maite decided not to have me ejected, but settled for one of her sternest looks whilst instructing me to remain silent.

At the end of the same meeting, as the audience dispersed, I was approached by a local man whom I knew to be the developer of one of the other Parcent PAI's. He stormed straight up to me and started prodding my chest. 'You are a foreigner,' he growled. 'Go home and keep your nose out of our politics.'

I'm not sure from where I summoned the courage, but in my best garbled Spanish I said, 'I am a citizen of Parcent. I pay my taxes here and that gives me as much right as anyone else to get involved in local politics.' (Or something to that effect.) It turned out to be another prophetic statement.

Chapter Seven

One of our favourite restaurants in Parcent was called La Tasca. It was a small establishment on the outskirts of the village with a tiny terrace at the front and a larger walled terrace at the rear. In the early days it operated like an informal French bistro, complete with gingham tablecloths and rustic artifacts hanging from the walls. There was no written menu and Celine would simply read out what was available on any particular day. This had two advantages: the food was always freshly cooked; and it didn't take long to decide which of the limited choices we preferred. The wine, always drinkable, came in earthenware jugs and was included in the price of the meal.

But then the proprietor, Pepe, decided to go up-market. The interior was redecorated, the rustic implements were replaced by chintzy prints and new suffused lighting was installed. Out went the paper tablecloths and serviettes to be replaced by linen, and the earthenware jugs were replaced with properly labelled bottles. Prices went up as well and Pepe was anxious to introduce a new, more extensive menu. Knowing of my interest in cooking, Pepe was keen to enlist my help as he wanted to include some dishes that would appeal to British tastes. Though saddened at the demise of the "old" La Tasca, I agreed to help and, if I say so myself, we managed to come up with some interesting options.

It was approaching New Year and Pepe was anxious to launch the new enterprise with a five course gourmet menu featuring a different wine with each course. To accomplish such an ambitious meal, Pepe decided to limit the menu to just two choices for the main. At my suggestion these were, breast of duck with a red berry sauce and, my favourite, a mustard and herb crusted rack of lamb with redcurrant sauce. Pepe was unfamiliar with the lamb dish and asked if I could provide him with a recipe. I was happy to oblige, especially as we had booked a table for four for the grand occasion.

At lunchtime on the big day, we were sharing a glass of cava with our house guests, Martin and Alison, who had arrived that day on an early flight from Gatwick. I was just whetting their appetites by running through the menu for the evening ahead when the phone rang.

'Mark, it's Pepe. We have a problem. Can you come down to the restaurant? Now!'

The kitchen was in chaos with huge pans already bubbling away on the range. Every single inch of work space was covered with vegetables in various states of preparation, and the four cooks (three specially drafted in for the occasion) seemed to be falling over each other and fighting for space.

'What's the problem?' I asked of Pepe, whose chef's whites were anything but white.

'Over here,' he said, leading me to the far end of the kitchen where a pile of lamb racks sat messily next to a huge bowl of something that looked like yellow porridge. He picked up a handful of porridge mix and slapped it on the back of one of the racks, but it immediately fell away.

'I just can't get the breadcrumbs to stick,' he announced.

The problem was obvious. 'Did you read the recipe?' I asked.

'Of course I read it, but I've never cooked this before. I have mixed the mustard and the herbs and the breadcrumbs, but they won't stick to the lamb.'

I realised then that I should have translated my recipe into Spanish.

'Pepe,' I said, trying not to sound condescending, 'what you should have done is mixed the dry breadcrumbs with the herbs, then you "paint" the mustard on the back of the racks and press this into the breadcrumbs.'

A look of exasperation crossed his face. 'Then we have a problem,' he said. 'I don't have any more breadcrumbs – plenty of herbs and a whole pot of Dijon mustard but no breadcrumbs.'

I should have just shrugged in that oh so familiar Spanish way, but I felt I would be letting him down. Besides, the crusted rack of lamb was my favourite and I didn't want to miss out. 'You have bread?' I asked.

'Yes.'

'And a food blender?'

'Yes.'

'Then what's the problem?'

'The problem, Mark, is that I am running out of time.'

I'd always fancied myself as a bit of a chef, but the last thing I wanted was to spend the run-up to New Year's Eve in a hot crowded kitchen. But that's exactly what I did for the next two hours – grinding bread into crumbs, painting forty-five racks of lamb with mustard and pressing them into the crumbs ready for the oven.

It was Martin's fault. He would insist on having a pre-dinner aperitif in the Cooperative Bar just up the road from La Tasca. It was packed, the service was very slow and we stayed for more than one. As a result we were the last to arrive at La Tasca. Pepe was there to greet us and show us to our table, beautifully decked with flowers and a Christmas candle. A waitress arrived with some tapas and the first selected wine. 'I'll take your order for the main course now,' she said, removing a notepad from the pocket of her apron.

I already knew the order – two duck and two rack of lamb.

She scribbled in her notepad and departed.

A couple of minutes later Pepe was hovering by our table.

'I'm sorry, Mark,' he said. 'We've had a run on the lamb and it's all been ordered, but there's plenty of duck.'

Perhaps it was the effect of the pre-dinner drinks, but I was in a cheerful mood. Some things are just not meant to be.

We finished the meal eating the traditional twelve lucky grapes, one on each stroke of midnight, ending up with the equally traditional mouthful of pips.

We were the last people to leave the restaurant and not without difficulty as Pepe had joined our table and plonked a bottle of Cardinal Mendoza brandy in front of us. I kept asking for the bill, but he kept saying it was too early to leave.

'Everybody said the lamb was excellent,' he said, rubbing salt into the wound.

It began with a phone call from a friend with links to the opposition party in the town hall – the *Coalició Democràtica de Parcent* (CDP). Would I be willing to put my name on their list of candidates for the forthcoming elections? I was flattered that they felt I could make a contribution, but what would Viv say?

By this stage Viv, having sacrificed a pair of her best boots, was as committed to the cause as I was. Even so, the thought that I might be catapulted into the corridors of power for the next four years was a step too far – for Viv as well as for me. Though my Spanish had improved no end, I was far from fluent and just could not see how I could cope with discussions and debates in the highly charged atmosphere of public council meetings. But I wanted to show my support for the CDP so I decided to accept an invitation to their first election planning meeting.

Ten o'clock was the appointed time – at night. At the last minute, the original venue was switched from the town hall for fear that it had been bugged. Then it was changed to the Social Centre before being switched again for the same reason. Eventually, I found myself in a rather grand town house on the edge of the village which apparently belonged to a CDP supporter and was undergoing restoration. At half-past ten eight CDP supporters gathered around a rickety table surrounded by a collection of equally rickety chairs set amidst piles of rubble and bags of cement. More stragglers arrived in the next half hour and business finally got underway around eleven o'clock. The CDP was an independent, non-aligned party, open to anyone who wanted to work for the village and defend the interests of all its citizens. Many of the people at the meeting were familiar to me as activists in *Veins de Parcent*.

The first item of business was to appoint the number one candidate on the list who would be *de facto* mayor (assuming we won the election). As they went around the table, one by one, all the attendees declared their reluctance to take on this responsibility. Great, I thought, some political party this is – they can't even agree on a leader. What I did not realise was that this attitude was indicative, not of an unwillingness to serve, but of a reluctance to appear ambitious. A leader, Manolo, eventually emerged and a fine and upright man he proved to be.

The meeting concluded at around two o'clock and I returned to Casa Emelia expecting Viv to be fast asleep. No such luck.

'Where the hell have you been until now? I was about to call the police.'

I had to explain that this was typical of the Spanish way of doing things. People had jobs and families, and late night meetings were the norm hereabouts.

'Do you want the good news or the bad news?' I asked.

'Whatever.'

'Well, the bad news is that I have agreed to be on the list of CDP candidates.'

'But you agreed…'

'The good news is that my name will be number seven on the list.'

I had to explain that the system of voting in Spanish municipal elections was based on party lists. The total number of councillors in Parcent was due to be increased from seven to nine that year, so each party would put forward a list of nine candidates and three substitutes. Seats on the council would be allocated pro rata to the percentage vote. This meant that at number seven on the list, I was unlikely to be elected unless the CDP had a landslide victory at the polls.

Over the next few months the clandestine meetings continued – always starting late and running on into the early hours. Manolo was always very kind to me, pausing to make sure I understood the discussions and asking for my views. This was a great education, not just in the Spanish language, but in getting to know the inner workings of local politics. I have to confess that I would have struggled without the presence of Joanna, a British woman who had lived and raised a family in the village over the previous twenty years or so. Joanna was actually number two on the list and in line to become deputy mayor – assuming…

Once a manifesto had emerged from our meetings it was time to present it, and the candidates, to the public. I attended several public meetings for members of the expat community to outline the CDP programme and answer questions. I did the same at a couple of meetings for the local population, speaking in Spanish from a pre-prepared script. I sensed there was suspicion at first, but I stuck to the line that I represented a group of foreigners who were not interested in their own finances, but who cared deeply about the future of the village.

I made many new friends from these rallies. People I hardly knew would stop me on the street for a chat and more gifts of fruit and vegetables began appearing on our doorstep. There were a few enemies as well, I noticed, as people with whom I had previously chatted, crossed the street to avoid me. Though I did not personally experience any direct ill will, it was clear that the village, at least the Spanish half, was split. Nasty rumours were spread and there were a few wanton acts of vandalism. Sadly Joanna and her family were prime targets, but they bore it with fortitude.

A break in election preparations gave us a chance to get away from Parcent and try somewhere completely different – France. With Jessie's passport duly stamped, we set off north for an overnight stay in a dog-friendly hotel in Figueres, famous as the home of Salvador Dalí. The next day we arrived at our ultimate destination – a *gite* attached to an old farmhouse located alongside the Canal du Midi at La Reole, in the Gironde Department of Aquitaine. It was a splendid place and the owners were kind enough to allow us and Jessie to use their garden so we could enjoy a picnic on the lawn.

Driving along the country roads in this part of France, it was interesting to contrast the neatly trimmed grass verges with the overgrown and shrivelled verges we had left behind in Spain. And this wasn't the only contrast we noted. Eating out was a completely different experience – not only was the food far more sophisticated than we had become used to in most Spanish restaurants, it was also far more expensive. Wine, included in almost every Spanish *menu del dia*, was an additional extra in France and, boy, did they know how to charge. And finishing a meal with coffee and a brandy, which was almost a routine in Spain (for me at least), could almost double the bill. However, this was our first holiday in years and we were determined to enjoy the change in culinary offerings.

We motored one day to the village of Saint-Émilion, home of the world famous wine, in search of some culture and a decent lunch. Quaint as the village was, it reminded me of places like Bourton-on-the-Water in the Cotswolds – a complete village museum where every other shop sold tourist items or the local wine at extortionate prices. After touring the scrubbed and polished cobbled streets, flanked by pristine stone buildings and newly whitewashed walls adorned with neatly trimmed hanging baskets, we set out in search of a spot of lunch. Sadly most of the eateries were well beyond our budget (even without wine) and so we decided to motor-on to somewhere a little less touristy.

Following the route of the River Gironde, we finally arrived in the city of Bergerac in the Dordogne. After circling the city looking for a suitable parking space, we eventually came to a halt in a small square with some shady trees where we could leave Jessie in comfort with the car windows open and within sight of the restaurant we had spotted in one corner. We paused at the entrance to the restaurant and studied the menu offerings. I was pleased to see several *"Prix Fixe"* choices ranging from a modest twelve euros to a more extravagant thirty euros. It was just before half-past one, Jessie was comfortable in the car, so I was really in the mood to splash out on some fine French food. I had set my heart on the four course thirty euro menu and was looking forward to a taste of haute cuisine.

We climbed the steps to the terrace and took our seats at a vacant table. Most of the other diners appeared to be just finishing their meals and it was almost five minutes before a rather surly waiter approached us. When I ordered drinks and asked to see the menu, the waiter haughtily raised his head and issued a deliberately audible tut before swivelling away and stomping back across the terrace. He returned a couple of minutes later and placed our drinks on the table together with the menu folder. Before I could examine it to make my choice, he reached over, opened the folder and turned each page in turn, pointing and uttering,' '*Non.*' (The thirty euro offering). '*Non.*' (The twenty-five euro option). '*Non.*' (The twenty euro choice). '*Non.*' (The twelve-fifty), before turning the final page and pointing to the two course *Menu Express* (nine-fifty euros) and announcing, '*Oui.*'

So much for our fine French lunch. In Spain we had become used to eating out at almost any time day or night, but in France it seemed that lunchtime did not extend beyond two o'clock. The lamb chops, sauté potatoes and peas arrived promptly and the waiter hovered at the side of the table, clearing the plates the moment we finished. The crème caramel arrived shortly afterwards, together with *l'addition* and we were ushered off the terrace before the clock struck two – without so much as a *merci beaucoup*.

Much as we had enjoyed our brief flirtation with la belle France, it was good to return to Spain.

Chapter Eight

Through many late night meetings, the CDP developed a manifesto for the election – a four page document with policies for everything from education to social services. There were policies for urbanisation, of course, which didn't rule out future building, but concentrated on linking existing development to the village – a matter of a few hundred houses, not thousands.

As a small local party, the CDP was strapped for cash and everything we did was paid for by voluntary contributions. Our manifesto was printed on a photocopier and as the election neared, we distributed it to every house in Parcent. Together with colleagues from our Association, we personally visited every expat in the village seeking their support. We discovered that many expats who were entitled to vote had not been registered, and so we embarked on a campaign to get them all signed up. It wasn't always easy and staff in the town hall put obstacles in our way, like refusing to help people fill in the necessary paperwork. Some prospective voters were put off by this, but we had a number of people proficient enough in Spanish to help them through the process.

With party funding, the Partido Popular was easily able to out-do us. In the week before the election they produced a ten page, glossy coloured brochure proclaiming their achievements over the previous four years and setting out their promises for the future which they claimed would all be funded from Valencia which was also in the hands of the PP. Amazingly, their glossy brochure contained not a single word about the three PAIs or the justification for wanting to urbanise millions of square metres of Parcent's beautiful countryside.

This, it turned out, was just the beginning of their obfuscation. A few days before the election we heard that Mayor Maite had been visiting expats telling them that the CDP was lying and that there were no approved plans for development; it was just an idea and everything could be discussed after the elections.

I hit the keyboard straight away and within twenty-four hours we were hand delivering a document in English and Spanish entitled '*La Verdad*' (The Truth) to every house in the village. It detailed every decision taken by the council in relation to the PAIs and invited readers to check the sources in the official council minutes.

Then we discovered that several family relatives of PP supporters had been included in Parcent's register of electors even though they were known to live elsewhere. Worse still, there were rumours that influential PP supporters were instructing their employees how to vote, claiming that they would be able to identify those who voted for the CDP and their jobs would be at risk. And business at a local gift shop run by a prominent CDP supporter suddenly dried up in the run-up to the election.

Was there no end to the PP's devious attempts to secure an election victory?

Between meetings and canvassing, I was approached again by Pepe from La Tasca to help him with his new menu. After the near disaster with the rack of lamb, I was nervous of making any more recipe suggestions, but it turned out he simply wanted help in designing and printing his new menus. I was not an expert in graphic design, but I had taught myself enough about a couple of computer programs to be confident that I could help.

Pepe said he had all his menu ideas written down in script and they just needed to be typed up and presented in a "professional" way. This was the easy part. I took away all Pepe's notes and his prices and returned the next day with a draft. That was when the problems began.

'Pork tenderloin with mustard sauce? – I can't possibly offer that for just 12.50 euros,' Pepe exclaimed.

'But that's the price you gave me,' I said.

'You'll have to change it – at least 15.00 euros, what do you think?'

I didn't think anything. It was his restaurant and his menu and I said so. So a first draft of La Tasca's new menu became a second and a third and a fourth until, finally, he agreed a proof copy and I printed twenty copies in both English and Spanish. These we inserted into the smart leather-bound folders which Pepe had bought specially for the purpose. It all looked very neat and professional, if I say so myself.

Pepe offered to pay me for my work, but I refused and we settled instead for the offer of a free meal when next we dined out at the "New" La Tasca.

It was a balmy evening and the terrace was

packed with diners.

'The new menu seems to be very popular,' I said to Pepe when he showed us to our table.

'Yes,' Pepe replied. 'We've been very busy. Now what would you like to eat?'

'Can we see the menu?' I asked.

'But surely you must know it off by heart. Take anything you want and don't worry about the cost. And I have a very special wine for you.'

Viv looked perplexed. 'Mark may know what's on the menu, but I've never seen it,' she said. 'Besides, I'd like to see what it looks like.'

Pepe returned with menus a couple of minutes later and the reason for his reticence was immediately apparent. Half the prices had been roughly crossed through with a felt tipped pen and new prices inserted in the same way. So much for all my efforts as an expert graphic designer.

The meal was splendid – Viv had the pork fillet with mustard sauce and I had the confit of duck with raspberries. The wine was excellent, too, a full bodied reserva from the Ribera del Duero, and followed by coffee and a Cardinal Mendoza brandy. I was feeling replete and more than satisfied when Pepe returned and joined our table.

'I'm glad you enjoyed the meal,' he said. 'Could you drop by on Monday morning? I have some new menu ideas I'd like to discuss.'

Well, I couldn't refuse could I?

Pepe's new idea was the addition of several traditional rice dishes available *por encargo* – to order. There was paella of course and *arroz a banda* (rice with fish) *arroz negro* (a black rice dish coloured with squid ink) and *arroz con morcilla* (rice with sausages). But there was something on the list I had never heard of – *fideuá*.

'What's *fideuá*?' I asked.

Pepe looked surprised. 'Call yourself a cook and you've never heard of *fideuá*? It is almost as famous as paella in these parts.'

The story goes that this dish was created in the 1920's when the cook on a fishing boat ran out of rice and used broken spaghetti or noodles instead to create a kind of sea food paella. It is said to emanate from the port of Gandia in the northern Costa Blanca and such is its popularity that each year a *fideuá* cooking contest is held in the city.

'My friend, Alfonso, won the silver medal last year,' Pepe said. 'He works at Restaurante Val de Pop not far from here in the village of Lliber. I'll take you there next week. You have to try *fideuá* and Vivien must come too.'

We arrived and took our seats. There was no choice as the *fideuá* had been ordered in advance. Now, it is worth stating at this point that Viv hates seafood. Fish, yes, but seafood, no. She could be tempted by a large prawn, so long as it is headless and peeled for her. She has savoured fresh crab sandwiches in Devon and Cornwall, but when it comes to what she would call "rubbery bits" they are simply out of the question.

The *fiduéa* arrived, steaming in a giant paella pan layered with inch long pieces of tomato flavoured noodles and topped with all manner of seafood. There were mussels and baby clams, slices of white cuttlefish and *chipirones* (whole baby squid) and a scattering of tiny prawns (complete with heads and shells). Pepe took charge of the large serving spoon and, ignoring Viv's pleas ('just a small portion, please'), heaped a veritable mountain of *fideuá* onto her plate before passing it across the table.

'Just eat the noodles,' I whispered to Viv as she fiddled and twiddled and diddled with the food mountain trying to find something she might design to eat. A small forkful of noodles did eventually make its way to her mouth inducing her face to distort to a pouting grimace.

'It's all in the stock,' Pepe said through a mouthful of noodles and seafood. 'It's made from fish heads.'

Viv excused herself and headed for the *servicios*.

'I don't think she's very hungry,' I said to Pepe as I scooped up another portion and sucked on a baby clam shell, which Viv contradicted by ordering a double helping of *tarte de manzana* (apple tart) for *postre*.

Chapter Nine

It is customary in Spain for elections to be held on Sundays and the Saturday before is deemed to be a day of reflection when no canvassing is allowed. So, on the final Friday evening, the CDP called a rally of all its supporters in Parcent's Social Centre. I was told it would be a very informal affair, mainly to thank supporters for their efforts.

When Viv and I arrived, together with some of our neighbours, the hall was already packed. Much to our embarrassment most of the Spaniards had brought plates of food and bottles of beer or wine. We had arrived with nothing. The food and drink was laid out on tables dotted around the room which meant that for most people it was standing room only. Then I noticed a long table and chairs set out at the end of the hall. As soon as we arrived, Manolo, our candidate for mayor, rushed to greet us and insisted I join him and the other candidates on this top table. My protestations came to nothing as I was told it was expected of me. Manolo made a short speech and then invited each of the candidates to speak in turn. Argh! – no prepared script. I muddled my way through a garbled message of sorts and to my surprise received a standing ovation – I think it must have been more for effort than for content.

With the formalities out of the way, the socialising began. Plates of food were thrust before us, wine and beer flowed and everyone seemed to be in a celebratory mood. I wondered if this was a sign of confidence, but when I asked around, the consensus was that the result would be very close.

My involvement with the *Coalició Democratica de Parcent* gave me an unusual insight into Spanish life – a view that most expats would be unlikely to experience unless, like me, they are drawn into the murky world of small village politics. For me it was an affirmation of everything I had come to know and love about the majority of Spanish people. My colleagues in the CDP were hard working and committed (as evidenced by the late night meetings that continued right up to election day). I thought my inclusion on the list of candidates might have been a token gesture; a means of keeping the expat voters on board. Far from it; at every meeting I attended they were at pains to ensure that I understood their discussions, setting aside their normal preference to speak in Valenciano (of which I understood nothing) and talking in Castellano (of which I had no more than a basic grasp). They were keen also to draw on my experience of local government and ask what I would like to see included in their manifesto. Many of my suggestions were taken on board, though my ideas for open government and greater public involvement in policy making proved to be just a tad too radical.

At one meeting, the issue of "councillors' pay" was discussed. In my naivety I had imagined there must be a standard set of allowances for councillors – a system with which I was familiar from my years in English local government. At first I thought the discussion rather unseemly until gradually I realised that elected councillors given a portfolio were actually required to fulfill their brief largely unaided. Apart from a Secretary and an office clerk, there was no paid officer corps to support the councillors and if things needed to be done, the councillors had to fend for themselves.

This particular point was illustrated to me some time later when I awoke one morning to find we had no running water. I spoke to my Spanish neighbour, Vicente, who had no such problem. It was a fiesta day (there are so many in Spain that they seem to occur at least once a month) so I knew the town hall would be closed.

'You need to speak to the mayor,' Vicente suggested.

'But the town hall is closed,' I said.

'So? You know where the mayor lives, go and knock on his door.'

I decided that my lack of water was not sufficiently urgent for me disturb the mayor on a fiesta day and the supply was reinstated early the next morning. But the incident spoke volumes about the difference between British and Spanish local government. It also explained why (with the notable exception of my colleagues in the CDP, I am sure) corruption in local administrations was rife. Almost weekly there were reports of mayors or other councillors being censured for corruption of varying degrees. Awarding contracts at inflated prices to friends or family was popular, as was taking back-handers for granting building permits or changing the zoning of a piece of land. The problem, it seemed to me, stemmed from a blurring of the roles of the executive and administrative functions. As a result, the checks and balances imposed by a clear separation of these roles were non-existent. Imagine a councillor responsible for specifying a service, inviting quotations or tenders, and then awarding the contract without recourse to any professional oversight, and you will understand the potential for malpractice. And the strange thing was that such practices seemed to be accepted with a degree of phlegmatic tolerance, perhaps a legacy of Franco's long years of omnipotent rule.

When voting day arrived, we stationed a couple of people outside the town hall (the only polling station) to act as tellers, counting in the voters we knew had pledged their support to the CDP. This is standard practice in UK elections, but it did not go down well in Parcent. Within minutes the local police officer, acting on instructions from Maite the mayor, was sent to move us along, alleging that we were canvassing for votes. In the end, an uneasy compromise was reached and we moved a few yards away from the entrance to the town hall. Then we heard that, at the urging of PP observers inside the polling station, some expats were being turned away because they did not have their passports with them, even though they had other proof of identity. (A phone call to the equivalent of the Electoral Commission soon rectified the situation.) By six o'clock we were missing quite a few promised voters so we began phoning round, urging people to come out and use their votes. Some gentle persuasion was needed to coerce people away from barbeques or from in front of the television; lifts were arranged for a few stragglers who claimed to be over the drink driving limit; and by close of poll at eight o'clock, all but a couple of our known supporters had been rallied.

The total electorate in Parcent was around eight hundred and fifty. The counting should have started immediately after the close of poll so we didn't expect to wait long to know the result, especially as there were only two parties involved. (The other national parties, in a show of solidarity with Parcent's extraordinary situation, had decided not to field candidates for fear of splitting the vote.) The counting was carried out by the same people who staffed the polling station and each of the parties was allowed to have an observer to oversee the proceedings. Each sealed envelope was opened and the voting paper was shown to the observers and then placed on one of three piles – Partido Popular, CDP or invalid. Every single vote was scrutinised by these observers with the PP seeking to find cause to reject them – especially if they were votes for the CDP.

As for me and the rest of the CDP supporters, we camped out in Bar Guay awaiting news. First reports, relayed by mobile phone, were not good – the PP was ten votes ahead. With half the votes counted their lead had increased to thirty. A mood of despondency descended on Bar Guay and muffled voices seemed to be considering the consequences of defeat. But then the mood changed. The PP's lead was falling to twenty and then ten and suddenly we were neck and neck. It seemed to be an age before the next news came through as a flutter of excitement spread through the bar. Ten ahead, twenty ahead. A loud cheer rang through the room as news spread – with just twenty votes left to be counted, the CDP was ahead by thirty and the PP contingent had stormed out of the town hall. That cheer was nothing compared to the eruption that occurred when, at around half-past eleven, the official result came through. The CDP had won the election by forty votes.

Corks popped, cheers rang out, the music began, impromptu dancing started, fireworks exploded in the street and the mother of all parties was underway. But the best was saved for the arrival of Manolo, the new mayor, who was cheered all the way along the street as he approached Bar Guay to be given a tumultuous welcome.

Tired, very happy, and very drunk (me at least) Viv and I staggered through the narrow streets of Parcent. Dawn was just beginning to break as we passed Hotel Casa Juliana, the planned venue for the PP celebrations which just happened to be owned by Isandro, the *ex*-councillor for *urbanismo*. The place was in complete darkness.

One of the novelties of uprooting and moving to another country is that you generally arrive knowing no one and with no one knowing you. Of course it is possible to actively seek new friendships, but often they simply occur through impromptu gatherings or shared acquaintances. Some remain just that – acquaintances, but others develop into more permanent friendships. And it is not always possible, on a first encounter, to predict how relationships might develop. My good friend Willie Boulton was one such a case in point.

On first appearance Willie was definitely not my type. Decked out in a fawn safari jacket with lapels covered in enamel badges, I imagined he must be a dedicated twitcher, an avid train spotter or perhaps a Friend of the Earth. But as ever, first appearances can be deceptive, for Willie was a gem of a man, annoyingly competent at anything he turned his hand to – a scholar and a gentleman one might say. He was a keen jazz musician, playing in a band at regular gigs in Javea and I first witnessed his small band at a concert organised in Parcent's Bar Guay. A raucous evening was highlighted by Willie's infectious enthusiasm, not only playing clarinet, but also singing in a voice that sounded remarkably like Sachmo himself, but without any hint of mimicry. Here was a man on a high with no more stimulus than the simple act of doing something he clearly loved. How I envied his childlike exuberance and zest for life.

One of his other talents was a gift for languages which he found incredibly easy to master. As well as being fluent in Spanish, he was a keen etymologist and would dabble in other languages just for fun. I once found he was planning a holiday in Greece and had started to study Modern Greek in preparation. I had no doubt he would be near fluent by the time he embarked on his vacation. It was as if, having mastered the mechanics of a foreign language, he was able to apply those basic formulae to any other language regardless of its ethnic roots.

Having got to know the man on a firmer footing, I was honoured to be invited to join a small group of "advanced" Spanish students at weekly classes he ran in the nearby village of Alcalalí. He was a hard taskmaster; a stickler for correct pronunciation with no time for shirkers or shrinking violets. But his lessons were always fun as he regaled us with tales from his past and homespun rules for remembering the correct conjugation of verbs.

But Willie's life was cruelly cut short. He had been diagnosed with an inoperable aneurysm, but determined to carry on and live his life as normal. Sadly, not long after the diagnosis, he collapsed and died on his way home from performing with his jazz band.

His funeral at a crematorium in Denia was an unforgettable affair. I had been to several crematoria in the UK and found them to be rather morbid places with dim lighting, funereal music and those heavy curtains that closed at the end of the service like a final cut-off point between this world and the next. In contrast, the crematorium in Denia was a modern purpose-built establishment, bright and airy with a vast stained glass panel behind the podium that depicted people of varying ages moving away towards a distant setting sun. There was no religious symbolism as such, just the sense of people moving on from this life to whatever lay beyond that sunset.

The place was packed to the rafters with two hundred or more people and the celebrants were entertained for almost an hour by snippets of Willie's favourite music, including one jazz piece recorded by Willie himself. The formal narration of Willie's life was interspersed with humorous anecdotes from many of his friends. The secular service was orchestrated by his wife and conducted in both English and Spanish in acknowledgment of the many

Spanish friends and neighbours in attendance. There were moments of poignancy, of course, but overall the occasion was one of fun and celebration, epitomised by the finale. One of Willie's jazz aficionados took to the podium and invited all present to join in singing one of Willie's favourite songs. And so we found ourselves part of an enthusiastic rendition of the Banana Boat Song.

"Come Mr Tallyman, tally me bananas. Daylight come and me wan' go home. Day-o, day-ay-ay-o."

I wasn't sure what the Spanish contingent thought of the performance, but the service ended with a rousing round of applause before we all filed out past the coffin (no curtains here) and paused for a moment's reflection. A fitting send off, I thought.

At the risk of being morbid I must just recount another funeral service we attended in Parcent. A long-term German resident had died after a prolonged battle with cancer and though the funeral itself had been a private family affair, there was to be a memorial service in Parcent's Catholic Church. The service was incorporated with the normal Thursday evening Mass attended by many of the regular Spanish church goers. They didn't seem to mind at all and maintained a respectful silence when the Catholic priest introduced a Presbyterian minister who spoke in German to present his eulogy. It said something to me about the gentility and tolerance of the majority of Spanish people I encountered.

Having won the election one might have imagined that those disastrous plans for Parcent would have been annulled at the first meeting of the new council.

But things are never as simple as that, at least not in Spain. To have annulled the plans arbitrarily would have left the new council liable to huge compensation claims from the developers. So the council merely asked the authorities in Valencia to return the plans to Parcent so they could be properly scrutinised and tested for legality. Even that action prompted criminal and civil proceedings against the new councillors, both collectively and individually. It took a further two years of wrangling, threats and recriminations by the (now opposition) PP councillors, before Valencia finally accepted the inevitable and ruled the plans should be annulled. Even so, threatened legal action by the Barrera Group hung over the CDP councillors for a further four years before finally being dismissed by the courts. And at the subsequent local elections the CDP increased their majority from forty to almost two hundred.

Chapter Ten

In the middle of that first election campaign Viv and I received an offer for Casa Emelia. It had been on the market for quite some time and even though the timing was awkward, we could not, as they say, afford to look a gift horse in the mouth. We had decided to sell for a number of reasons, none of them related to the threat of development as, by that stage, we were confident the plans would never be progressed. In truth, Viv never settled there; the garden was too small; she disliked the open plan lounge/kitchen; and the novelty of setting and cleaning the log fire (our principal source of heating) had long since worn off. In addition to all this, we had both failed to appreciate the consequences of living outdoors for more than half the year and the effect of living so close to all our neighbours. It wasn't that any of them were unreasonable, indeed we were friendly with all of them, but it is impossible to block out extraneous noise and, being less tolerant than most people might have been, we had decided to move to somewhere more isolated, with more land and *central heating*.

Having accepted the offer on Casa Emelia, we began to scour the estate agents for the right place. We were very reluctant to leave Parcent especially since we had made so many friends there, but we just could not find the right property in or near the village. So, with a deadline looming, we began to look further afield. We found our ideal place on the outskirts of the nearby village of Lliber – an ancient *finca* (farmhouse) much restored and reformed, located on the edge of the vineyards with magnificent views across the valley to Jalon and beyond. We could even see Parcent's church spire in the distance. There were no immediate neighbours (at least none within spitting distance) and it came with almost four thousand square metres of land including an old stone ruin. It had the benefit of double glazing throughout, central heating and, above all, it was constructed on protected land and therefore free from the threat of further development nearby.

Much as we missed our friends in Parcent and our sense of belonging in the community, it was something of a relief to be away from politics and controversy and arguments and acrimony and the rest. I promised Viv faithfully that I would stay away from the town hall and keep my nose out of local politics. In short, we vowed to start our retirement all over again and that's exactly what we did.

Our first day in Finca Romero was not, however, without its problems. Because the purchasers of Casa Emelia were anxious to complete at an early date, and because Finca Romero was not immediately available, we were forced to rent a small villa for a couple of months. Our furniture was held in storage by a removal company in Benissa and when we finally visited the Notario to complete the purchase, it was simply a matter of making a phone call to the removers to have everything delivered to our new home. Well, that was the theory.

One drawback of moving to somewhere more

remote immediately became apparent. The bumpy old track that led to our new home did not appear on any maps and certainly not on any satellite navigation system. For all intents and purposes Finca Romero did not exist. With Viv waiting at our new home, I was busy cleaning up at our rented villa when my mobile phone rang. It was the removal men and they were lost. I tried giving them directions over the phone but it was hopeless, so I phoned Viv.

'I know they are lost,' she said. 'I can see them from the pool terrace and they've been going round in circles in the vineyards for the last twenty minutes. I've been waving at them frantically, but I just can't attract their attention.'

I suggested that Viv phone them direct in their van and she did just that, talking them in as she waived from a distance. But that was not the end of our removal problems. One of the things that impressed us when we first viewed Finca Romero was the rather grand entrance with two stone pillars supporting a pair of double wrought iron gates at the end of a private driveway. What I had not realised was that the driveway was relatively narrow and the two stone gate pillars supported a large wooden beam which formed a kind of pergola. When I eventually arrived back at the house, the furniture removers' pantechnicon was stalled at the top of the drive unable to enter the front garden because the beam was too low. What's more, with a sheer drop on one side and a rocky outcrop on the other, it was impossible to off-load from the back of the van and carry the items up the side. The driver and his mate, already exasperated after their unscheduled excursion around the vineyards, were now spitting feathers.

'Why didn't you tell us about the beam?' the driver said. 'We could have made two trips in a smaller van.'

It seemed rather lame to tell them that I hadn't noticed it when we bought the house. The solution, which was not without its own problems, was for the van to reverse back down the drive, turn round and reverse back up again so they were at least near to the gates. Even so they were not best pleased at having to carry everything some forty metres from the gates to the front door, especially on a gloriously hot June day. I helped as best I could, carrying box after box into the house, each of them carefully labelled by Viv with their destinations clearly marked – dining room, kitchen, lounge etc. – and I swear that some of them were the same boxes we had removed from England some five years earlier and still unopened. It reminded me to remind Viv that we seriously needed to de-clutter.

Finca Romero is a characterful old pile. One wing comprises an original stone *casita* with walls almost two feet thick (over a hundred years old according to the estate agent) whilst the remainder is of more contemporary Spanish construction – breeze blocks and cement render. Though no one starting from scratch would have designed such a quirky layout, it somehow seemed to work, giving us a blend of old and new with rustic beams, arches and alcoves combined with double glazing, modern radiators and air conditioning. There was also a separate building adjacent to the main house in the form of an old *riu rau*. These two arched constructions are typical hereabouts and would have originally been open-sided and used for drying grapes to make raisins. A previous owner had glazed-in the arches to form a storage area which doubled as a games room. There was consternation on my part when Viv announced it would make an ideal formal dining room, not least because we rarely dined formally these days. But the biggest drawback was that the old *riu rau* was not connected to the rest of the house and could only be accessed from the kitchen by crossing a walled courtyard.

'What happens if it rains?' I said. 'The roast potatoes will go soggy and the gravy will be diluted.'

But the dining room furniture had travelled with us all the way from England, so it had to be housed somewhere. There was no other space in the house so Viv had her way. 'Besides,' Viv said with portentous logic, 'it hardly ever rains in Spain.'

We had been in our new house about three months when the summer came to its usual abrupt end with a torrential downpour. Though providing welcome relief for the garden, the storm had a couple of unexpected consequences. The first was a flood in the dining room. The walled terrace which sloped down toward the old *riu rau* terminated in a shallow gulley running in front of the entrance door and connecting to an overflow pipe which ran beneath the floor. What we had not realised was that during that summer this overflow pipe had become blocked with an assortment of dried leaves. As a result, the excess water poured out of the gulley and under the door. We awoke to find our dining furniture sitting in a two-inch pool of water – not the best thing for the mahogany veneer on the mock Chippendale. Luckily the Chinese rug had not been laid otherwise it, too, would have been floating in the murky water.

The second consequence of the storm was a lightning strike that penetrated our telephone cable, breached the surge protector, fried our broadband router and sizzled the motherboard on the computer. I can only put this down to a lack of proper lightning conduction in the telephone network. We learned a very expensive lesson – disconnect the telephone jack when there are storms about, even if it meant going into temporary isolation from the rest of the world. Perhaps because of the storm we encountered another technical telecommunications problem. Every time it rained, or there was drizzle in the air, the telephone line died. As soon as the rain stopped and the sun returned, the line would reinstate itself. This led to several interesting conversations with the call centre that handled line faults. Located somewhere in Latin America (I swear I could hear the Atlantic Ocean crashing in the background) the conversations went something like this.

(From my mobile phone) 'Hello, our landline is dead.'

'OK, thank you for reporting it. Our engineers will respond within forty-eight hours.

(Call to our landline) 'Hello, it's the telephone engineer here. We have a report of a fault on your line, but it seems to be working now.'

'Yes, that's because it's stopped raining and the sun is shining.'

'Well, if it's working now, there's nothing we can do, so we'll report the problem as resolved.'

(Two days later from my mobile phone) 'Hello it's me again. It's raining and the landline is dead.'

(From the other side of the world) 'Thank you for reporting the problem, our engineers will respond within forty-eight hours.'

'Yes, but it will probably have stopped raining by then.'

'Our engineers will respond within forty-eight hours.'

The problem persisted for most of that autumn until I managed to persuade the telephone engineer to give me his mobile number so I could call him direct the next time it rained. Finally this worked and Paco (we were on first name terms by this stage) came out in the middle of a shower to diagnose the problem. There was a break in the insulation covering the above-ground cable which meant water was penetrating the line. When the break was identified the problem was quickly resolved by patching in a new section of cable. But this only solved the problem temporarily as within weeks another section had perished and then another. After four or five repeated episodes, Paco concluded that the whole length of cable was shot and needed to be replaced. What I had not realised was that our house was so remote that we were the only people at the end of a five hundred metre length of cable stretching across a dozen or more telegraph posts back to the village. Paco returned the next day with a colleague and they spent a whole day climbing up and down the posts, stringing up a complete new section of cabling – problem solved, at last, and we didn't have to pay.

Such things are sent to try us, but they are not

without frustration. If you are happy and content with life in Spain, then it is easy to take these things in your stride.

'What's a day without the internet?' I would say to Viv. 'So the electricity has been off for six hours now – there's nothing worth watching on the television anyway. I can still cook something nice on the gas hob and we can have a romantic candle-light supper.'

Viv withstood such tribulations stoically, though perhaps with a lesser degree of sang-froid than me. An inability to use the washing machine for a day was, apparently, something approaching a crisis.

Of course, if you had already joined the ranks of "Hacked Off in Spain," then every episode of minor disruption became a calamity of disastrous proportions. For me they had to be taken in the round, together with the gentler pace of life and less stressful existence I generally enjoyed. In truth, I was, I think, becoming more Spanish and learning to cope with adversity with the same degree of phlegmatic patience which was manifest in the Spanish psyche.

So burst water pipes, which became a regular feature of our lives, were just another minor annoyance. And like so many other things in Spain, the root cause could be put down to poor materials or workmanship, or both. At our old house in Parcent we suffered several leaks in the main supply pipe running from the water meter to the stop-tap inside the former garage. The general rule was that leaks occurring on the house side of the meter were the responsibility of the owner. So I dealt with the problems myself by digging down through the gravelled drive to identify the leak and then patch in a new section of pipe. The cause of the problem was immediately apparent – the plastic pipe had been buried just a few centimetres beneath the surface without conduit or any other kind of protection; just covered with a thin layer of stony earth and gravel. Bear in mind that this was the drive to the house, crossed daily by our car, and it is easy to understand why the pipe fractured with monotonous regularity. When I made the fifth or sixth such repair, I finally concluded that the whole length needed to be replaced, protected by a sturdy conduit, buried to a greater depth and covered by a layer concrete. Another little project to fill my time.

When we moved to Finca Romero I imagined all such problems might be behind us. Wrong. The previous owners had obviously suffered similar problems and I discovered that a new length of water pipe had been inserted between the meter at the bottom of the drive and the gates at the top – a distance of some forty metres. But rather than bury the pipe in the rocky ground, they had simply laid the new pipe over-ground, threading it between the bushes as if to hide it away. The effects of this make-do solution were twofold. In the summer we had endless supplies of free hot water as the pipe was heated by the scorching sun. This was ideal for showering outdoors, but not so good when it came to washing salads as we had to run the cold tap for about five minutes to obtain anything resembling cold water. In winter we had the opposite effect. When temperatures dropped below freezing, as they did on many clear winter nights, the pipes froze and we were without water until the sun rose and thawed them out

– usually around midday. A small inconvenience, I thought, until Viv pointed out that she could not operate the washing machine without running water.

One of the joys of living in Finca Romero was the uninterrupted view across the vineyards that stretched almost as far as the eye could see. But living with such a view was not without its drawbacks. It was not a single commercial vineyard, but a patchwork of privately own plots each just a half acre or less. Some were expertly cultivated, others less so, and a few were totally overgrown and neglected. This private ownership meant there was a small army of farmers doing their bit, accompanied by a fleet of small tractors and *mula mecánicas* constantly chugging across the landscape. A few plots were still cultivated by horse or mule-drawn ploughs.

Through most of the autumn and winter the landscape appeared barren and brown as the sleeping vines shed their leaves and recuperated from the energy-sapping effort of producing the previous year's crop. It was February before the cycle started again in earnest as the stubby stock branches were shorn of last year's fronds. In recent times, the favoured instrument for this shearing was a pair of hydraulic powered secateurs which released a sound not unlike an air rifle as each frond was cut back to the stem. With up to twenty fronds on each vine and a hundred or more vines to each plot, it was not uncommon to wake to the sound of secateurs snipping away for hours at a time. Having given the vines a short back and sides, the surplus material was gathered to one end of each plot to be burned. Our breakfast on the terrace was frequently accompanied by the scent of wood smoke as our vista disappeared in a sea of smoky mist that lingered in the bottom of the valley often until lunchtime.

The next process was weed killing. This brought men in spacesuits with backpacks which they pumped with a lever as they meandered up and down between the rows. Ploughing followed, as the narrow-gauge tractors meandered between rows of vines and broke up the rich red earth. March and April brought a short respite from intense activity as new fronds gradually began to emerge, turning the view from bare brown to fresh green. The blossom came next, filling the air with a pungent sweet scent until it faded to reveal embryonic bunches of grapes. And now battle commenced. To prevent mildew and attacks by insects, the new growth had to be dusted with sulphur. This generally involved placing the fine powder in a hopper on the back of a tractor which was connected to a large fan-like contraption. The result was a vast billowing cloud of yellow powder which, depending on the weather and the wind direction, dispersed in somewhat random fashion and occasionally in the direction of Finca Romero. The same was true of the liquid copper sulphate, dispersed in much the same way and giving off plumes of blue mist. We did sometimes wonder if living in such close proximity to the vineyards was as healthy as we had first imagined.

By September it was harvest time with most of the grapes being destined for the cooperative bodega in Jalon. The boss of the bodega would routinely visit vineyards in the region and test the grapes for ripeness and sugar content. When a particular zone was "called in," an army of workers would descend like a swarm of bees. Though many of the harvesters were the families of plot owners, others were itinerant workers moving from plot to plot. As the heat of the day peaked at around two o'clock, the families departed for home and the itinerants sought shade for their siesta. But shade was hard to find in the vast swath of low-growing vines, so the workers sought out the nearest clump of trees – which just happened to be a small copse of prickly oak trees at the bottom of our drive. So it was that we regularly found a group of half-a-dozen South American types dossing beneath our trees. They were harmless enough and quite friendly, especially when we offered them bottles of cold water. They usually repaid us by leaving behind the detritus of their lunch – half-eaten bocadillos, plastic bags, cling film, tinfoil and empty drinks cans.

The grapes were stripped by hand, each bunch carefully cut away and then carried in heavy rubber buckets to be tipped into a trailer lined with plastic and attached to the back of a tractor. The tractors then joined the traffic jam of similar vehicles heading for Jalon. By October the vines were ready once again for their winter rest and we, too, enjoyed a peaceful respite from the frenetic activity of spring and summer.

Despite the drawbacks, the flat vineyards, criss-crossed by a series of agricultural access roads, were ideal walking territory for Jessie who was getting on in years. We enjoyed many such walks, following the seasons and observing the grapes' annual life cycle from close quarters. But sadly our beloved Jessie died just a year after we moved to Lliber. She had reached a good age for a German shepherd and slipped away peacefully in our arms. She is buried in the garden with a view over the vineyards to Jalon and Parcent in the distance.

'No more pets,' we both said, and meant it. After thirty years with an assortment of German shepherds it was time for us to enjoy our freedom and do some travelling.

Our first excursion was a long weekend in Madrid. We found a splendid hotel on the magnificent Gran Via, known as the Spanish Broadway. Once famous for its many theatres, it is now a Mecca for shoppers – or more aptly, Heaven, as Viv would describe it. It was March and we had travelled prepared for the cold and winds to be expected in Europe's highest capital city. At an altitude of 21,000 feet it is renowned for hot summers and cold winters affected by breezes from the surrounding sierras. We arrived in the middle of a springtime heat-wave as the sun shone brightly and the breezes stayed away. We found ourselves mingling with the sun bathers stretched out on the banks of the lake in Retiro Park and eating al fresco in the Plaza Mayor.

We visited the Prado Museum to be overwhelmed by room after room of walls dripping with paintings by Goya, Valàzquez, Rubens, Titian, El Greco and Bosch. A single afternoon is simply not long enough. I made my own personal pilgrimage to the Reina Sofia Museum to see Picasso's Guernica. Viv was distinctly unimpressed, but I was simply mesmerized by the enormous black and white canvas and its gruesome depiction of the after-effects of the first recorded aerial bombardment by German and Italian planes in 1937.

Food is always a priority for me and I had done my research beforehand to identify one "must visit" restaurant called Botin, tucked away in a side street through the arcades of the Plaza Mayor. It is reputedly one of the world's oldest restaurants and the wood-fired ovens in which the food is cooked are said to have been in continuous use for more than two hundred years. It was Saturday night, but this was March so we didn't expect the restaurant to be busy and I hadn't made a reservation. As we turned the corner in Calle Cuchilleros, we found a long queue of mainly America tourists snaking out of the restaurant and along the street. Much as I wanted to eat at this august establishment, I have never been good at queues, so I pushed my way through the throng to speak to the maitre d' (or whatever the equivalent is in Spanish) and tried to book a table for the following night.

'Not a problem, sir,' he said. 'What time would you like?'

'About eight o'clock?'

He sucked his teeth. 'That's a little early. Later is better.'

'Nine?'

'Ten or ten-thirty would be better,' he concluded and we settled for that. No wonder Madrid has a reputation as the city that never sleeps.

We settled that Saturday night for another restaurant just around the corner from Botin. My earlier research had identified a speciality of Madrilenian cuisine to be *cordero lechal*, which translates as milk lamb, but in effect means baby lamb. I've never been squeamish, at least when it comes to food, so this was an ideal opportunity to sample a local delicacy. But there was a problem. *Cordero lechal* was only available for a minimum of two persons and Viv is most definitely squeamish when it comes to eating fluffy little animals.

'Young, old, what's the difference?' I said. 'A lamb is a lamb. We eat spring lamb in England and I can't imagine this will be much different.'

Wrong!

A small trolley was wheeled alongside our table. It was topped with a silver salver covered by a dome. The dome was removed to reveal a half a baby lamb – not the front half or the back half, but the whole right side (it might have been the left side, but I didn't pay that much attention) split down the spine from head to tail. And when I say tail, I mean tail, as Viv squealed at the sight of a short curly thing protruding from one end. The waiter, who was adept at serving this particular delicacy, proceeded to split the carcass down the middle using only a fork and a spoon.

'Which piece would madam prefer?' he asked.

It was a no brainer.

I can only speak personally, but the meat literally fell off the bone and melted in my mouth. Viv, however, seemed to have more of a problem swallowing her portion.

The following night, we finally made it to Botin. It's a vast establishment comprising innumerable small rooms dominated by ancient beams and individual fireplaces and spread over four floors connected by rickety stairs. I settled for the house speciality of *cochinillo* (suckling roast pig) which was as melt-in-the-mouth as the previous night's lamb. Viv opted for salmon, despite the waiter's raised eyebrows. At the end of the main course I felt the need to make use of the facilities (as they say in polite circles). I was directed out of our small dining room, along a narrow corridor, up the stairs, along another corridor up more stairs to the top storey. Getting there was fine, but on the return journey I became disorientated in the rabbit warren of stairs and corridors, and a wrong turning placed me in the kitchen amidst an army of cooks and waiters.

'I seem to be lost,' I declared, stating the obvious. 'Can you tell me where my room is?'

A waiter escorted me back to our table where Viv declared, 'I thought you'd got lost.'

'Lost? Me? As if?'

On our final day in Madrid we had a morning to kill before departing for the airport. Viv was intent on some last minute shopping and I trailed along unenthusiastically wondering, not for the first time, just how many pairs a shoes a woman needs. And then I spotted it – a small open-fronted restaurant shoe-horned (excuse the pun) between the shops; its walls decorated with gaudy tiled murals that were presumably all the rage around the turn of the century. But what really attracted my attention was a metal brazier placed to one side of the entrance. It was pierced with holes through which I could see the coals glowing amber and on top.... a large paella dish full to the brim with yellow rice, chunks of meat, peppers and a scattering of prawns.

I know that paella originated in Valencia, and Madrid is a long way from there, but, hey, paella is a national dish these days and Madrid is in Spain.

We were seated within minutes with Viv grumbling about the loss of shopping time. When it came to ordering, there was simply no choice, was there?

If I had paid more attention in my pursuit of the perfect paella, my suspicions might have been aroused by the absence of steam rising from the paella. If I had given the brazier a closer inspection, I might have realised that the coals were imitation glass, illuminated by an electric light bulb topped with a small fan to give the effect of shimmering flames. But it was still a surprise when the waiter took two plates to the front of the restaurant, scooped out two portions of cold paella, then returned to place these in a microwave oven and wait for a "ping."

The search continued.

Walking through the vineyards it was easy to see the evidence that wild boars were frequent visitors to our neighbourhood. The soft earth was often indented with hoof prints, roots had been grubbed up, and the stone *bancales* which buttressed the vine terraces were frequently disturbed, leaving large rocks strewn across the narrow *caminos*. One of our Spanish neighbours referred to them as *una plaga* (a plague) and I wondered why, since hunting was a national pastime hereabouts, more weren't shot for food. Vicente explained that many of the animals were diseased and before they could be eaten, they needed to be tested by a vet. That, together with the cost of butchering the carcass, meant that supermarket pork was generally preferred, even if it was bland in comparison to the gamey flavour of the wild boar.

We rarely saw the beasts themselves as they were nocturnal and we were reluctant to walk through the vineyards at night-time. Then, in the early hours of a still, dark night we were rudely awakened by a thunderous clattering that seemed to be coming from the roof.

'Quick,' Viv said. 'It's a thunderstorm. You need to disconnect the telephone cable or the computer will get fried again.'

Dazed as I roused from a deep sleep, I fumbled for my slippers and dressing gown and headed down the hall. It was then I realised the noise *was* coming from the roof and it was moving from one end of the house to the other. As I opened the front door, I heard a roof tile crash to the ground. As I rounded the end of our bedroom and looked up, there, silhouetted against a pale moonlit sky, was a full-sized wild boar staring me straight in the face. My first reaction was to scarper for fear it might jump down and attack me. But I summoned the courage to clap my hands and yell, prompting the boar to turn-tail and race back along the roof, dismounting at the back of the house and running off into the distance.

I should explain at this point that the oldest part of Finca Romero was cut into the side of a rocky outcrop. This meant that at one point it was possible to step onto the roof from the footpath which ran along the back of the house. And though our front garden was secure, the ruin plot at the back of the house was open to the surrounding countryside. The next morning as I surveyed the damage and set off to the builders' merchant to buy twenty new roof tiles, Viv announced, 'And you'd better enquire about fencing off the rest of the plot as I don't fancy bumping into any more wild boars on our land. Either that, or you'll have to buy a shotgun.'

Another little project to occupy my time.

Despite our skirmish with the powers-that-be in Parcent, it always fascinated me, as a former local government officer, that all of the villages in the valley each had their own town hall and their own elected council. My first thought was that these councils might resemble a typical Rural District Council in the UK, with powers which covered little more than the village pond and a few benches in public parks. But even with populations of just a thousand inhabitants, local Spanish councils have a full range of powers from planning to social services, schools and libraries – even if the purse strings are firmly in the control of Alicante or Valencia.

Convenient as it was to pop along to the local town hall, I couldn't help thinking that it would surely be more cost-effective to amalgamate them all into a single administration covering the seven or eight villages dotted around the valley. But, I was to discover, such talk was tantamount to heresy. Each of the villages had their own identity and this was fiercely guarded and maintained. I would almost go so far as to suggest that there was an intense rivalry between the villages, and not just in the flamboyance and extravagance of their local fiestas.

As far as I could gather, the only joint venture operated by the villages was a central refuse collection contract. Even then we were constantly urged only to use the refuse bins in our locality because the council was billed by weight for everything collected in its area. This led me, mischievously, to the thought that if I placed my refuse in the bins in the next village it might reduce our IBI (council tax) bill.

Every village had its own primary school, some with fewer than fifty pupils. Surely such small numbers would have meant closure or amalgamation in the UK. I did wonder about the quality of education on offer, especially when some of the schools were overwhelmed by an influx of non-Spanish pupils. But I came to the conclusion that having a school within walking distance overrode all other considerations.

Each village had one or more dedicated local policemen/women whose duties ranged from school crossing patrols, to collecting market fees, to planning enforcement.

Most villages had their own library as well, though these generally comprised just a single room with a meagre selection of books, and opened for just a few hours each week.

By far the most absurd illustration of this parochialism arose when the authorities in Valencia stumbled on the idea of recycling centres – what would once have been called the council tip. Every small council was invited to bid for one of these quaintly named "Eco Parks." At least three of the local villages were successful in obtaining funding for the construction of concrete hard-standings on which to place a series of receptacles for different materials. Within a couple of years, Parcent, Jalon and Alcalalí each boasted a local Eco Park with grand signage proudly announcing funding from the Generalitat de Valencia and the European Union. However, a problem arose because the funding only covered the capital costs and nothing had been set aside for day-to-day running costs. Since most of the local councils were strapped for cash (or possibly starved of revenue from the regional or provincial authorities) there was only one solution. The facility in Jalon opened for just a few hours on Wednesday and Saturday mornings, Alcalalí opened on Tuesday afternoons and the Parcent Eco Park never opened at all. And woe betide anyone from Jalon who tried to use the facility in Alcalalí or vice versa. As residents of Lliber, we were at least permitted to share the facility in Jalon, though we were required to give our name and address and the attendant always made a note of our car registration number. It all worked perfectly, if you were Spanish, but I couldn't help thinking that one Super-Eco Park at the centre of the valley would have been a much more practical solution.

As regular visitors to Spain will know, the Spanish love their hoardings and signs, and not just the commercial advertisers. Governments at all levels love to announce the fact they have promoted or funded particular initiatives. Typically these signs would remain in existence for years after the projects were completed, presumably as a reminder of good deeds and in the hope of garnering support come election time. One risible example of this practice came to my attention when the traffic in Lliber was temporarily diverted whilst a couple of workmen mounted a large, two square metre, hand-painted metal sign to the side wall of the village's social centre. The sign announced, *"Reformación y Redecoración"* and stated that the project was funded by the Diputación de Alicante. When writing numerals, the Spanish convention is to use full stops where in Britain we would use commas and vice versa. So, as I studied the newly erected sign I found it difficult at first to comprehend the figures – 1.835,76 euros. Surely they were not about to spend over a million euros on refurbishing the village's two-room social centre. It took me a while to work out that the sum involved was 1,835 euros and 76 cents, and I couldn't help wondering what proportion of that cost had been swallowed up in painting and erecting the monumental sign.

Sometimes, having a local town hall and local councillors does have its advantages. The narrow gravel road to Finca Romana which wound its way for five hundred metres through the vineyards, was frequently prone to flooding and generally pock-marked with deep potholes. Together with my Spanish neighbour, Vicente, and a few other people who used this road, we made several attempts over a couple of years to fill the depressions with loose gravel. This improved the situation, but only until the next storm.

One autumn afternoon, I was pottering in the garden when a large wagon stopped just outside Vicente's house and began to off-load a consignment of steel reinforcement bars. There were enough for an industrial sized construction, and my first thought was that Vicente must be planning something big. When the lorry departed I wandered down the drive for a chat.

'They're going to concrete the road,' Vicente said.

'But when?' I asked.

'They start in the morning,' Vicente explained. 'You won't be able to use the road for a couple of days.'

'Well, it's good of the town hall to let us know,' I thought, but said instead, 'I thought the town hall didn't have any money.'

'They don't,' Vicente said, 'but my son was elected to the council last May and Alicante has stumped up the money.'

What it is to have friends in high places.

The village of Senija, just a kilometre or two from Lliber was one of those unremarkable linear settlements we passed through on the way to somewhere else. A couple of bars, a tobacconist and a restaurant were the most notable features of the main street. We occasionally availed ourselves of the Friday offering of fish and chips at Bar Nou. Apparently someone had given Rosa-Marie a recipe for batter which she recreated with reasonable success to provide crispy hake, decent chips and frozen peas. The offering also came with tartar sauce or, for the heathens amongst us, tomato ketchup.

Like so many of these villages, there were hidden gems to be found if you were prepared to explore on foot. A butcher's shop, a bakery, a church and a small square were tucked away from the main road, along with a couple more small restaurants.

Exploring one day, I happened upon a place called Mama's with a bland frontage that barely stood out from the adjacent colour-washed houses. I might normally have passed by without interest, but something caught my eye – a small sign in the window announced: "*Paella para llevar.*" Could they really be serious? Take-away paella?

I mentioned this oddity to our friends Pat and Les who were surprised at my ignorance as they had tried the take-away paella before. Well, this was one experience I just had to try. Les made the arrangements and ordered a paella for four to be collected at precisely one o'clock one Friday. Pat and Les arrived at our house early, in time for an aperitif, and then Les and I set off for Senija, just a five minute drive away.

I had been imagining foil packets with cardboard lids and plastic forks and wondered if there would be one big container or four separate portions.

'It's almost ready,' Paquita said. 'Just five minutes. Would you like a *caña* while you are waiting?'

Two small wine glasses of beer, barely a couple of gulps, appeared before us and we finished these just as Paquita appeared from the kitchen.

'*Está listo,*' she said as she hauled the giant paellera up onto the bar, still sizzling and loosely covered in baking foil. We paid the princely sum of thirty six euros (the *cañas* were free apparently) and carried the pan to place on an old blanket in the boot of Les's car. As I said he had done this before.

'*Conduce con cuidado,*' (drive carefully) Paquita

said. '*¡Buen provecho!*'

Another excellent paella, and still remarkably hot when we removed the foil to release the steam and the aroma of garlic and fried chicken. And all the more enjoyable for being eaten with friends in the shade of our terrace overlooking the vineyards with the mountains in the distance. The only drawback? – the washing up. We were obliged to wash the paellera and return it to Paquita, 'Whenever you're ready,' she said. 'Anytime in the next couple of days.'

Which made me think. If Paquita had a sudden rush of takeaway orders, how many paelleras did she have in reserve?

Chapter Eleven

Our pet-free existence had lasted more than six months, but apart from our brief sojourn in Madrid we never really fulfilled our commitment travel and see more of Spain. And knowing of Viv's fondness for animals (at least of the domesticated variety) I should have realised that the status quo would not last forever.

It was my fault. On one of my regular trips to the *Mas y Mas* supermarket in Jalon, I spotted this ginger and white cat sitting boldly on the broad pavement immediately outside the automatic front doors. He was something of a celebrity in the locality and seemed quite content as customers would regularly buy him food and leave the opened cans for him to help himself. Viv had long since eschewed the weekly shopping trips – 'Spanish supermarkets are so boring, give me Marks and Spencer any day,' – so it was left to me. I really shouldn't have said anything, but I let slip that I had seen this cat busking for food.

'It seems quite happy – and fat,' I told Viv.

'But it must be cold. And where does it go at night? And what about stray dogs and the traffic?'

Strangely enough, Viv joined me on my next shopping trip and several others thereafter and we always came away with tins of luxury cat food. It seemed reasonable to indulge her so I never once complained about the expense.

A couple of weeks later as we returned from

meeting friends in Jalon, Viv interrupted our drive home saying, 'Oh, I've just remembered, I need to stop off at *Mas y Mas.*'

'Dinner's in the oven,' I said. 'What on earth do you need at this time of night?'

'Just pull up outside and I'll pop in. I won't be a moment.'

I did as instructed.

Before I could say anything, Viv had stepped out of the car and scooped up the cat. 'Just drive,' she said, like some latter-day bank robber (or kidnapper).

Mickey had arrived at Finca Romero and within days he decided that lazing around in the lap of luxury beat busking for a living. And within weeks there was no doubt about who was boss around the house as Viv directed me, 'Don't sit there, that's Mickey's chair.' I knew my place.

The time came for the annual general meeting of the Sector Repla Residents Association in Parcent of which I was now ex-President. As the most controversial issues were now out of the way, it was decided to make this more of a social gathering with a brief meeting followed by lunch. The venue was to be Parcent's famous paella restaurant, L'Era, which was renowned across the region and visited by Spaniards from Valencia and further afield. Surely this was my opportunity to sample an authentic paella Valenciana.

I had long since realised that a paella for one or two people is a rather miserable affair. It can be done, yes, but the whole tradition of paella demands a larger gathering of people able to participate in the act of sharing food from a communal pan. With some thirty attendees seated around a table running the length of the restaurant, we were in for a truly Spanish experience.

The fare on offer at L'Era is rustic to say the least. It comprises a starter bowl of salad shared between six or eight people – nothing sophisticated here just lettuce covered with roughly chopped tomatoes, sliced onions and olives, served with crusty bread and alioli. The main course is the paella which is cooked over wood-burning stoves and served in sooty-bottomed paelleras about the size of a dustbin lid. This is followed by a communal bowl of fruit which, depending on the season, comprises whole apples, oranges, pears, bananas, chunks of melon and/or watermelon, a bunch of grapes, a peach or a few apricots and perhaps a wedge of pineapple. One peculiarity of L'Era is that all three courses – salad, paella and fruit – are eaten from a single small plate and using the same cutlery throughout the meal. Of course, this saves on the washing up, but I gained the impression that this was more a custom than a labour-saving innovation.

The wine, included in the ten euro cost, is served in plain bottles without labels – a gutsy red or pungent white. Coffee, if ordered, is accompanied by a complimentary glass of *mistela*, a kind of sweet fortified wine made from the local grapes found throughout the Jalon Valley.

Though there are other dishes on the menu, almost everyone opted for the paella which came in two varieties – a meat version or a mixed version with meat and seafood. For some reason, most people at our gathering had expressed a preference for the meat version and so, when it came to be served, four large paellas were delivered and spaced along our table for everyone to help themselves.

So, what of the paella itself? There was rice aplenty, flavoured with a rich garlicky broth, dotted with bony pieces of chicken and rabbit and chunks of diced belly pork. The vegetables comprised sliced runner beans, red peppers and butter beans. I had no doubt it was authentic and probably all the better for not being tarted up as so many old rustic recipes can be. In short it was very tasty indeed, especially as they had managed to create the all-important *socarrat*.

If this explanation of the L'Era experience tempts anyone to search it out, the restaurant opens every day (except Wednesdays) and only at lunchtime since no self-respecting Spaniard would eat paella as an evening meal.

Having fenced off the ruin plot at the back of Finca Romero to prevent further intrusion by wild boars, it was time to turn my attention to the ruin itself. I call it a ruin since it was little more than a collection of roofless, crumbling walls showing the footprint of a collection of outbuildings which I suspect were once attached to the original stone-built wing of our house. Imagine Tintagel Abbey ruins but on a much (much!) smaller scale. I doubted the ruins had ever been inhabited, more likely they had been used for the storage of agricultural produce, equipment and machinery. There might even have been stabling for a donkey or a horse. The estate agent who sold us the house said the ruins had "development potential" though he clearly had more imagination than me. Besides, we had been warned by our lawyer that any further building on our plot was likely to be prohibited as the land was now zoned as *protegido*.

One section of these ancient walls did, however, give cause for concern. It was a length of about six metres and some four metres in height which in effect formed a retaining wall against the rocky outcrop into which it had been cut. A narrow pathway ran along the top and back of the wall and gave access to the rest of the plot. The problem was that over the years a substantial section of this wall had toppled to the ground, and the top pathway was gradually being eroded to the stage where it was virtually impassable without risk to life and limb. Luckily, all the original rocks used in the construction of the wall lay in a heap at the bottom, so there was no shortage of material for reconstruction.

There is frequently confusion, at least amongst expat residents, in relation to planning regulations in Spain. Most people (though not everyone) would understand you must obtain permission from the town hall to build or extend a house. But not everyone realises that, technically at least, any works on property (laying a patio, building a garden wall, etc) need a *licencia de obras* (licence for works). I was not sure that reconstruction of part of a ruin fitted the definition of *obras* since I was merely putting back what had fallen down. Besides, there was a fee to be paid for a licence, so I decided to take a chance in the belief that our house was remote enough to mean that no one would ever notice.

With the stones already in situ, all I needed for my

latest project was a few cubic metres of sand and a dozen or so bags of cement and these were duly ordered-up from the local builders' merchant in Jalon. The lorry arrived early the next morning and managed to reverse onto the plot through the double gates I had thoughtfully installed in the recently erected fencing. Within five minutes, as I stood by the mountain of sand and wondered if I might have over-ordered, Francisco, the local village policeman (*Policia Local* not *Guardia Civil*) pulled up in his official car at the side of the gates to enquire what I had in mind. I explained the project and he promptly announced, 'You need a *licencia de obras.*' I couldn't really argue. I later discovered that there was an arrangement (if not an obligation) for builders' merchants to notify the local police of any substantial deliveries of construction materials.

The next day I obtained the necessary *solicitud* (application form) from the town hall and brought it home – all four pages. I managed, just about, to answer all the questions and prepared a plan of the ruin along with some photographs of the crumbling section and a satellite view taken from Google Earth. The final question on the form asked for an estimate of the cost of the work and explained that the fee for the licence would be two and a half percent of the cost. Since the only cost to me was the sand and cement, I answered honestly – two hundred euros.

The clerk in the town hall told me the application would have to be considered by the architect. As the architect only worked for a few hours each Friday this would take about two weeks. Four weeks later, and still with no news, I made an appointment to see the man himself. I arrived in good time and was asked to take a seat in the town hall foyer. I could hear voices from the open-plan office at the top of the stairs, but twenty minutes later I was still waiting. Finally the clerk said to me, 'The mayor is with the architect, but why don't you just go up, otherwise you could be here all morning.'

The mayor, with whom I had a nodding acquaintance, greeted me with a handshake and asked what I wanted. When I explained, the architect, sitting on the other side of the desk said, 'What application? I don't remember seeing any application.'

'But I submitted it five weeks ago.'

Perhaps embarrassed by the mayor's presence, the architect began to shuffle through an overflowing filing basket.

'That's it there,' I said, recognising the yellow folder into which I had inserted the *solicitud*.

He pulled it out and began to thumb through the pages and then, with a sharp intake of breath, he announced, 'There could be a problem. This is protected land.'

At this point the mayor intervened. 'Let me have a look.'

As the mayor turned the pages I entered my pleas.

'I'm simply repairing an old piece of wall, using the existing stones with a bit of sand and cement. It's dangerous, you see, and every time it rains more of the wall crumbles away. If I do nothing the whole section might topple over. Look at it this way, the ruin is over a hundred years old and I'm trying to conserve a piece of local history.'

The mayor eyed me suspiciously. 'You're not

planning to put a roof on it?'

'No, of course not. I just want to repair the wall and remove the danger.'

The mayor turned to the architect and said, 'Give him the licence.'

A week later I received a phone call asking me to call in and collect the document. The clerk handed me the paper and said, 'That will be ninety-seven euros.'

I protested, 'But the cost is just two hundred euros as I'll be doing all the work myself. Two and a half percent of that is next to nothing. How do you arrive at ninety-seven euros?'

'Even if you do the work yourself, the fee is based on what the work would cost if you employed a proper tradesman. The architect has done his own estimate of the cost and the fee is based on this.'

I couldn't say anything as the rebuilding project was already well on the way by this stage. So I paid up and smiled nicely.

Of the project itself all I can say to anyone contemplating a similar enterprise is – start with the big stones at the bottom, because climbing up ladders to place huge stones at a height of four metres is not to be recommended. Small wonder that a year or so later I was recovering in a Benidorm hospital after undergoing an operation to rectify a double hernia.

My minor skirmish with the *policia local* over the *licencia de obras* was easily resolved and in the end I was happy enough to comply and pay my dues. Indeed, as law abiding citizens, we always did our best to comply with the law of the land even though the law itself was not always that clear. On first arrival in Spain it is often difficult to distinguish between fact and rumour when it comes to compliance with Spain's myriad of rules and regulations, not to mention the interminable bureaucracy. Added to that, there is any amount of (usually misleading) advice from fly-by-night expats who are happy to take a chance on the grounds, either that nobody really cares in Spain, or that they were unlikely ever to be caught out.

Being more assiduous than many, and not wanting to fall foul of the *Guardia Civil* who have something of a "shoot first and ask questions later" reputation, we opted for compliance. We had already registered and obtained our *numeros de identificación de extranjeros* (Foreigners' Identity Numbers) which are essential in order to open a bank account or buy a house. Next we registered on the *padron* at the local town hall since this is both an obligation and a pre-requisite of voting rights. Soon after this we went through the process of re-registering our British car (endless paperwork, correspondence between Spain and the DVLA in Cardiff, a trip to the British Consulate in Alicante and four hundred euros). We procrastinated over whether to apply for residency, but as the law is clear if you are living in Spain for more than half the year, we set the process in motion. After more form filling, photographs and finger printing and another trip to Alicante, we finally obtained our *tarjetas de residencia* complete with mug shots and fingerprints. This credit card-sized document came in handy on many occasions and meant we were relieved of the obligation to carry our passports at all times. (A note here – the *tarjeta de residencia* has since been replaced by a simple paper certificate which is not nearly as useful as proof of identity, especially as it does not include a photograph.)

Our next step was undertaken, not so much as an obligation, but as a piece of self-interest – we applied for eligibility for the Spanish health service. I must confess to having some misgivings about this as it required certifying to the UK authorities that we no longer wished to claim on the British NHS. Nevertheless, after more form filling and a trip to the social security office in Denia, we were finally registered with our local GP and entitled to free medical care and reduced prescription charges. (Another note here – to be eligible for a Spanish SIP card – *tarjeta sanitaria* – one or both of a couple must be in receipt of a UK state pension unless you are working and paying Spanish national insurance contributions.)

By this stage we were almost fully compliant with all aspects of Spanish law, with one exception – our driving licences. There is much speculation, and even more rumour, about whether a European driving licence is valid for a UK resident in Spain. In our case, however, the situation was clear since both our driving licences were of the paper variety and issued in the UK. As residents of Spain we needed to apply for Spanish driving licences. Perhaps it was laziness or form-filling fatigue, but we never quite got round to this and, as dictated by Sod's Law, this particular chicken came home to roost.

On our way to Javea one morning (to fill in our tax forms, I might add) I was driving unhurriedly along the N332 when I was flagged down by an officer of the *Guardia Civil* and directed into a lay-by to join a queue of other motorists. As we awaited our turn to be interrogated by one of three officers dealing with the queue, I couldn't help noticing the guns in their holsters and pondering on their fearsome reputation. I was trying hard to remember a piece of advice I had been given to always use the polite (*usted*) form of the second person singular of the verb when talking to the Guardia – to use the informal (*tú*) verb form would be seen as a gross impertinence and probably lead to summary arrest.

'What's the problem officer?' I enquired in my best Spanish through the open car window when my turn came.

'You were speeding,' he stated brusquely.

I was puzzled since I knew the standard speed limit on a national highway was 80 kph and I was sure I had not exceeded this. The officer was kind enough to confirm this, but also pointed out that on this particular stretch of road, the presence of a road junction joining from the right meant the limit dropped to 60 kph – and didn't I see the sign?

I apologised profusely, hoping my contrition might spare me further interrogation.

'*Permiso de conducir,*' (driving licence) he demanded.

Now I knew I was in trouble and I was beginning to regret my decision to speak in Spanish – pleading ignorance of the language might have been preferable. My particular problem was that the car was Spanish registered, I had Spanish residency, but only a UK driving licence which was not valid in my circumstances. I just hoped he might assume I was a tourist and decided not to volunteer the fact I was a resident, hoping instead to bluff it out.

'I only have my English driver's licence,' I said, producing the document for his inspection.

He began scribbling in his notepad.

'Numero de Identificación,' he stated.

This I knew off-by-heart and recited it for inclusion in his notes.

'I need proof of identity,' he added, *'pasaporte?'*

As I had a residency card I no longer carried my passport, but of course I did not want to admit to being resident.

'I don't have my passport with me,' I said.

'I need proof of identity,' he repeated.

Viv, following the conversation from the passenger seat, decided to help out.

'Why don't you show him your *residencia*,' she said.

At this point I noticed the hand-cuffs dangling from the officer's belt.

Certain that he had heard Viv's remark, I extracted the *residencia* card from my wallet and passed it to the officer almost adding – 'it's a fair cop,' and offering my wrists in anticipation.

He scribbled some more, returned my card and then tore away a sheet from his pad and handed it to me.

'The fine is ninety euros,' he said, 'but there's a discount of twenty euros if you pay within fourteen days.'

I was just wondering if I should slip him few euro notes to pay there and then when he added, 'You can pay at any of the banks listed on the back.'

As I started the motor to move away, he offered me a sympathetic shrug and then spoke to me in English. 'It's just routine – orders. Drive carefully.'

A few weeks later we were the proud owners of new Spanish driving licences, which was just as well because…

Since our house did not appear to exist on any map, our post was delivered to a room adjacent to the social centre in the village of Lliber where we had a private post box. Opposite the social centre there was a small lay-by, and whether we collected our post generally depended on whether there was a parking space. On one particular day I set off for Jalon with our household rubbish in the car, ready to deposit in the appropriate receptacles located at the edge of the village. The lay-by for the post box was clear, so I pulled over and popped in to collect a bundle of letters. Now, I always wear my seat belt in the car; it's a habit I am happy to have acquired. However, on this occasion, as the rubbish bins were just forty metres ahead and just around the corner, I made a conscious decision not belt up. Sod's Law was at work again. As I turned the corner, I was confronted by another green-uniformed *Guardia Civil* officer, his hand raised, instructing me to halt.

'*Cinturón de seguridad*?' he barked.

What could I say? I apologised profusely and explained that I *always* wear my seat belt, but as I had just collected the post (I waved the bundle of letters) and as I was heading for the rubbish bins (I pointed to the refuse bag) which were now just ten metres ahead of us (I pointed them out) I had "forgotten" to put on my seat belt.

Without smiling he waved me on with a message. '*Siempre* (always) *ponga el cinturón de seguridad.*'

Relieved, and thinking that perhaps the Guardia's fearsome reputation was undeserved, I wound up the car window, engaged first gear and prepared to drive the ten metres to the bins. Before I had moved an inch, he tapped on the car window. I disengaged first gear and wound down the window. The officer's face distorted to a scowl. '*Lo que te he dicho,*' (What did I tell you) he said quietly. And then, raising his voice, '*Ponga el cinturón – siempre!*'

I obeyed, of course, and then drove to the bins, removed the seat belt, deposited the rubbish, replaced the seat belt and moved on, relieved that my new driving licence was still without penalty points.

Everything comes in threes, and so it was with my encounters with the Guardia Civil. Returning home late one morning on the narrow road near Alcalalí, I turned a corner to be confronted by another green goblin holding his hand aloft and directing me into a lay-by.

'What have I done this time?' was my first thought as I pulled off the road. I was just a couple of hundred metres from the turn-off to home.

The officer walked towards me and ordered, 'Stay there.' Then he stepped into his patrol car and drove off.

Was he going for reinforcements? I thought. Or sending for a prison van?

The cause of my enforced delay soon became apparent. The peloton of a bike race, some thirty riders, flew past in a blur of colour, closely followed by a group of support cars complete with spare wheels strapped on roof-racks. Less than a minute later another group of perhaps fifty cyclists and four more support cars chased by. Another minute passed and a further chasing group came by, then another... and another. Then nothing. I waited for five minutes wondering if the Guardia would come back to release me. After another five minutes I was about to start the car when a group of three stragglers cycled by. I remained in the car as a lone cyclist cruised by, seemingly in no particular hurry, followed by another loner two or three minutes later. Still I waited until, finally, another support car appeared which I presumed to be bringing up the rear. By this time I had been stationary in the lay-by for almost half an hour. Surely all the racers must have passed by now. I gave it another couple of minutes then decided to gun it home. I had travelled a distance of just fifty metres when I rounded a bend to be confronted by a another lone cyclist, looking somewhat distressed, and followed by... a Guardia Civil car, blue lights flashing.

'Oh dear,' I said to myself (or something similar) as I slammed on the brakes and came to a halt in the middle of the carriageway.

The cyclist passed by and then the police car came to a halt at the side of my car. The officer wound down the car window and I felt obliged to do the same to allow the ingress of what I can only describe as an official rant including a few expletives I would rather not repeat here. He drove on, leaving me chastened but relieved not to be heading for the local nick as I drove, very slowly, home.

Chapter Twelve

Viv spent much of her leisure time tending to our extensive garden – and reflecting ruefully on the differences between gardening in Spain and in Britain. True, she no longer had to battle with the winter storms or rake up tons of fallen leaves for compost. And rarely was she confined indoors by inclement weather. But that didn't mean gardening was easy. In the summer, the rich red earth set like concrete and daily watering was an absolute essential if tender new plants were to survive the summer scorching. We learned by expensive trial and error; plants that flourished in pots at the garden centre were not always easy to sustain. And it wasn't just the summer drought that caused problems. Finca Romero, situated at the very base of the valley, was in a well-known frost pocket as the cold air rolled off the surrounding mountains and settled somewhere just outside our house. When selecting new plants we learned to enquire if they were frost hardy, to which Armando at the garden centre would reply, 'Normally yes, but you live in El Pla de Lliber, so I can't guarantee it.'

As well as the vagaries of the weather, there were other, more serious, threats to Viv's efforts to cultivate a colourful flower garden. Even that emblematic Mediterranean plant, the humble geranium, was not immune as it was attacked by the geranium moth (*Cacyreus marshalli*) said to have arrived in Spain from the African continent. The caterpillars from these grey-brown moths burrow their way into the stalks and then munch away until the stalk is dead. We tried every proprietary spray we could find, even following a suggestion of spraying with garlic crushed in water which was supposed to ward off these predators, but nothing worked. Viv even tried following the moths with a fly-swat, but I was never sure which caused the most damage – the moths or Viv's frantic (and usually ineffective) swipes. By the end of each summer, our prize geraniums were generally reduced to just a few stubby shoots which were barely worth saving.

Our single palm tree also presented no end of problems as the dreaded palm weevil (*Rhynchophorus ferrugineus*) invaded Iberia. We had read warnings about the devastating effect of this giant red beetle, but it was only when we noticed several dead palm trees in our vicinity that we began to take the threat seriously. By that time it was almost too late. It was Viv who first noticed the problem when she called me over to listen to our palm tree – yes, listen. As we stood in silence at the base of the tree we could literally hear the sound of munching, as the beetles' larvae chomped their way through the tender new shoots at the heart of the tree. Armed with a chemical from the local agricultural cooperative, I mounted the ladder and sprayed ten litres of liquid into the heart of the palm and repeated the operation a week later. The chomping stopped, but when we came to trim away the dead fronds, evidence of the invader was plain to see as several new shoots were perforated with holes about one centimetre in diameter. And as I cut away the decayed material I found several large cocoons, about the size of my little finger and made from palm fibre, embedded in the heart of the tree. The tree survived, just, but the problem persisted and we were advised to spray at least monthly during the spring and summer months. Gardening can be such a chore.

Whilst Viv maintained a constant vigil and sustained a relentless battle with the predators, I moved my attention to the ruin plot. I had harboured a long term ambition to grow my own vegetables on our extra land. With the ruin successfully restored, I set about turning the ground in preparation. The land immediately below Casa Romero is rich, red and fertile, but our land, which is slightly raised from the vineyards, is quite different. Every time I wielded a spade, a mattock or even a pick axe, all I struck was solid rock lying beneath a thin covering of soil. Eventually, by trial and error, I managed to till enough ground to create four small vegetable plots ready for planting, though at the end of the process I had enough loose rocks to rebuild another section of the ruin. The soil I uncovered was dry and stony, devoid of nutrients, and before planting I decided a good dose of manure would help things along. In England it would have been relatively easy to source farmyard manure or horse manure from local stables, but since I had never seen a farm (in the English sense of the word) or anything approaching an equestrian centre, it was never going to be that easy.

Armed with the Spanish word for manure – *estiercol* – I began to ask around. Most of my enquiries prompted nothing more than a shrug of the shoulders with an accompanying expression of puzzlement that seemed to say, 'Why does this English idiot want to buy manure?'

Undaunted, I pressed on and finally Raul at the builders' merchants gave me a lead. Hidden away in the hills on the southern side of the valley was a farm where I might be able to buy *estiercol de toros* (bulls' manure). He wasn't sure of its exact location, but gave me rough directions. Following these, I crossed the river in Jalon and continued down the road alongside the riverbed before turning left and winding my way up into the hills until the road petered out. I had arrived a La Paloma, a breeding centre for bulls which, I was to learn later, supplied the animals for the ritual bull running that formed the centerpiece of all the local village fiestas.

As I pulled into the yard I could see in the distance a herd of a fifty or more young bulls grazing peacefully on the foothills. As I meandered through a ramshackle collection of outbuildings, I was suddenly startled by a thunderous thud against some heavy vertical planks. The planks formed a corral of sorts within which was enclosed the kind of angry, stomping bull I imagined rampaging across a bull ring inflamed by a waving cloak. Between the planks, I could see a glistening black coat and, as the massive beast turned, its long pointed horns thrust forward colliding with the timber which rattled in its frame. A closer glance brought me into direct eye contact and the bull seemed to give me an angry sneer as it snorted through flared nostrils dripping with mucus. It was then I looked down at my red T-shirt. As I tried to figure out the shortest escape route, a voice rang out.

'¿Que quiere?'

What I wanted was to leg it out of the place and never come back.

'I'm looking for *estiercol*,' I said to the portly gent in grubby denim dungarees tucked into a pair of dirty wellington boots.

He removed his sweat-stained baseball cap as he approached me and a smile crossed his stubble-encrusted face. 'You've come to the right place amigo,' he said clamping an arm around my shoulders and ushering me away from the corral.

'I can buy *estiercol* here?' I asked as we crossed the yard.

'Hombre si. ¡Por supuesto!' (Of course!)

We rounded an open-sided barn piled high with shredded carobs destined for fodder. They were festering in the heat and emitted a sweet musty odour that made me gag. The man led me to the back of the barn where I was confronted by an enormous heap of dung which, though dry on the surface, was nonetheless discharging a full head of steam.

'How much do you want?' the man said, wafting an arm toward the heap.

I must confess that, to this point, I had not really given this much thought. My initial idea of filling a few bags to put in the back of the car had not met with Viv's approval, so I was not sure what to say.

'I'm not sure,' I said. 'I don't have a trailer.'

'I can deliver in a lorry if you like, as much as you want.'

'Well, yes, a small lorry load would be fine.'

He pointed to a short flat-bed wagon parked on the edge of the yard. With low boarded sides I imagined the wagon could accommodate one or perhaps two scoops of manure from the shovel of the tractor parked alongside. This was more than I felt I needed, but I had come this far so there was no point in scrimping on the job, was there?

'I'll dig some out from the bottom of the pile,' the man said. 'It's well-rotted and ready for use straight away.'

We haggled over a price (fifty euros including delivery) and he asked where I lived. Knowing that our house did not exist as far as cartographers were concerned, I started to give him directions. He nodded in understanding as I described the route to Finca Romero. When I finished, he smiled knowingly and said, 'Your neighbour, he is called Vicente, yes?'

'Yes, you know him?'

'He is my cousin. I had lunch with his family only last week. I know your house very well.'

On the way home I congratulated myself; everything was going brilliantly. How many other expats could have tracked down a source of natural manure and negotiated door to door delivery?

'It'll be here this afternoon,' I told Viv when I returned home. 'Eduardo, he's Vicente's cousin you know, will be delivering it personally in his lorry.

'I hope it doesn't stink,' Viv said, unimpressed by my excitement.

Just after four o'clock that afternoon Eduardo sounded the horn of the lorry to announce he was nearing the house. I left Viv indoors poring over the gossip columns of the Daily Mail and dashed round to the ruin plot at the back of the house. As the lorry began to reverse through the double gates, I blinked in disbelief. Eduardo had thoughtfully added a series of metal stanchions to the side of the wagon into which he had slotted a series of wooden planks, thereby increasing the height of the wagon and its overall capacity. Worse still, the steaming manure was piled high, even above the height of the sides.

'It's too much,' I protested to Eduardo to which he replied, 'It's good stuff, you can never have too much. You'll have the best vegetables in the valley.'

Astounded, I watched as the bed of the lorry was elevated to tip the contents onto the ground. I stood back in amazement at the sight of my very own mountain of *estiercol de toros*.

'It's arrived, then,' Viv said as I returned to the house.

'Er... yes, but there's rather a lot of it.'

As Viv stood before the steaming pile, I expected her to say something about, 'a load of old bull shit' but she settled for saying, 'You'd better get a tarpaulin and cover it up before the flies start to swarm and the neighbours complain.'

Even a liberal dosing of *estiercol* on my small vegetable patch failed to make a dent in the mountain and I resorted to telling all my friends to come and help themselves – 'It's free so long as you provide your own transport.'

Most common fruit and vegetables are readily available in season in the local markets and they are generally very cheap. But try buying figs in January or mangoes in March and you'd be out of luck. Even the Spanish supermarkets tend to concentrate on seasonal produce and you would have to visit a speciality shop to find the more exotic produce out of season – and pay the price. So, in my efforts at home growing, I decided to concentrate on some of the hard-to-find items. That spring and summer we had an abundance of mange tout peas, spring onions, purple sprouting broccoli, rocket, Swiss chard and basil. And though tomatoes are readily available, I cultivated some more exotic varieties – golden yellow and black cherry. The problem, as most home-growers will testify, was that everything ripened at once and I gave away almost as much as we used ourselves. That, combined with the constant battles against snails, caterpillars and mildew, made me think more than once if it was worth the effort. But I had inherited my father's green fingers and so I was hooked.

As we approached our first winter in Finca Romero it was time to try out the central heating. After freezing our socks off in Parcent, we were looking forward to discarding our thick woollies and thermal underwear. We did indeed luxuriate in the warmth of the radiators and reacquainted ourselves with the novelty of simply turning up the thermostat. Alas, this comfort lasted all of three days before the boiler started playing up and we were left without any heating whatsoever.

The previous owners of the house had kindly left details of the company who had installed the boiler and were certified to carry out service and repairs. They were based in Gandia, a city some fifty kilometres away, and they did not have a local agent. 'Don't worry,' they said when I called them, 'one of our engineers will call in the next time they are in your area.' We waited... and waited. Three weeks later, having retrieved the thermal underwear, a service engineer finally arrived.

Forty-five minutes later, Hilario presented us with a bill for one hundred and fifty euros and announced, 'I've given the boiler a full service and there was air in the system so I've bled the boiler and all the radiators. It's working fine now.'

It did indeed function perfectly and we were warm as toast... for the next three days. This time when I examined the boiler (housed in a lean-to at the side of the dining room) there was a plume of steam rising from the top and a steady trickle of water seeping from the bottom. I'm no expert, but it was obvious to me that the boiler was unsafe so we switched it off and called Gandia once again... and waited. A further three weeks passed, as did several increasingly acrimonious phone calls, and by this stage we were approaching Christmas. It wasn't my fault, but that didn't stop Viv complaining as she wrapped herself in a blanket on the sofa and caressed a mug of hot soup.

Time for action. My premonition was that when (if) Hilario ever returned, the likelihood was that he would need a spare part or some such thing which he would have to order, so the chances of us being warm for the festive season were slim at best. It wasn't in the budget, but we decided to replace the boiler – but with less than ten days to go could this be achieved?

At ten o'clock next Saturday morning, I sat in the office of Juan Blazquez, *Fontanero* of Alcalalí. I like to support Spanish tradesmen whenever I can, not least because most of the British fly-by-nights had returned to Blighty when *La Crisis* began to bite. But my familiarity with the Spanish *mañana* culture did not fill me with confidence. So it was with a degree of skepticism that I listened to Juan as he promised, 'If you order now and pay a deposit, I will install the new boiler on Tuesday.'

True to his word, Juan and his assistant arrived on time and by the end of the day we were basking in the radiant heat of fully functioning central heating and finally looking forward to Christmas. I asked Juan about the bill, but he said he was busy and it could wait until after Three Kings. We finally paid up in the middle of January after I had chased Juan on several occasions to present his invoice. A true gent, Juan, and when, several months later, he delivered several lengths of copper piping, joints, solder etc. to our house, he was anxious to know what I had in mind. I explained that I was extending our water pipes under the rear terrace to provide an outdoor tap for the purpose of watering the new vegetable plot.

'Who is doing the work?' he enquired.

'I'm going to do it myself,' I explained.

'You are *fontanero?*' he asked.

'No, but it's just a few bits of pipe and soldered joints. It can't be that difficult.'

Juan puffed out his cheeks and shrugged. 'I'll be round later to inspect your work,' he concluded. And when, a couple of weeks later, he popped by the house, he declared himself satisfied with my workmanship (except for an excess of solder on some of the joints – better safe than sorry, I say) and offered to take me on as his apprentice. Eat your heart out Lord Sugar. I declined of course. 'I hate plumbing,' as I had said to Viv on many occasions and would no doubt have cause to say again in the future.

The central heating functioned perfectly over Christmas and into the New Year, but it seemed to be guzzling oil. A glance at the gauge indicated we had less than a hundred litres left – by my calculations, enough to last about ten days. I contacted a local supplier, Gasorba, who were happy to fulfill my order for eight hundred litres except… We were approaching Three Kings on 6th January and they were closed to business for the next four days. Three Kings came and went and still no delivery – there was a backlog they said. Down to our last few litres, I was becoming desperate, not least because Viv was threatening to move into a hotel. I pleaded with Gasorba and finally they agreed to deliver on the following Saturday morning. We might just last out until then if we turned the thermostat down.

Bearing in mind the previous difficulties with deliveries to our house (that low beam at the gate) I had specifically told the assistant in the office that we needed their small oil tanker. I also explained the problems in locating Finca Romero and left instructions that the driver should call when he was nearing Lliber so that I could meet him in the village and he could follow me home. The driver duly called to say he was on his way and I arranged to meet him on the main road at the entrance to the vineyards. As I waited, looking up the hill that dropped down into the valley, I spotted him in the distance and flashed my car lights. He flashed back in acknowledgement and I began to drive down the *camino*. It was only when he turned into the road that I realised he was driving a full-sized oil tanker. I should have stopped him there and explained, but what could I do? Viv already had her bags packed.

As the driver halted, confronted by that low beam, I noticed he was thumping the steering wheel and uttering all kinds of incomprehensible Spanish expletives. My efforts to explain, 'I asked for the small lorry,' did nothing to appease him as he continued his rant. Then, looking at the height of the tanker and the height of the beam, I suggested he might just make it underneath. This only prompted further ravings as he explained that whilst he might just scrape through, by the time he had discharged the load, the lorry's suspension would rise and he might not be able to get out. Neither of us wanted that.

'Where's your oil tank?' he fumed at last.

I showed him and he paced out the distance – about forty metres. In silence he stomped back to the wagon and began unravelling the hose, dragging it across the gravelled terrace to find it just reached our oil tank with about one metre to spare. I'm normally quite a chatty person and I like to practice my Spanish at every opportunity, but as the man blithely puffed on a cigarette whilst filling the tank, I decided to retreat indoors for the ten minutes it took to fill up and reel in the hose. I thought of explaining the health and safety implications of his actions, but I had no wish to expand my knowledge of colloquial Spanish. I paid the man, giving him a hefty tip (which he barely acknowledged) and left him to reverse the tanker down our narrow driveway. As I have said before – such friendly people, the Spanish, always tolerant and helpful. Perhaps I just caught him on a bad day.

Having rescued Mickey from destitution on the streets of Jalon (according to Viv, that is) we had effectively reneged on our vow of no more animals. 'In for a penny, in for a pound,' has always been one of Viv's mottos, so it wasn't long before she began to take more of an interest in the abandoned animals section of the local newspapers. There are so many unwanted or abandoned animals in Spain that the rescue societies (usually operated by well meaning expats) had resorted to aggressive advertising in the local press. There was usually a full page at least of cute photos accompanied by heart rending stories through which every shape and size of animal pleaded for help.

'Hi, my name is Gunther, I'm a two year old Rottweiler. My owners left me for hours chained to a tree in the garden with no food or water until I was rescued. I'm very clean and fully house-trained, but a little boisterous. I love children (and not just for breakfast) and all I need is a safe warm home and plenty of food. I promise not to chew your furniture if I get regular walks to burn off my excess energy.'

'Yes, but does he like cats?' I said to Viv as she studied the cutie-pie photo with tear-filled eyes. (Viv's, that is, not Gunther's).

It had to happen.

'Hi my name is Gesa. I'm a three-year-old white German shepherd cross. It's the second time I've been abandoned and I've been locked up in this sanctuary for almost six months now. All the bigger dogs bully me and I'm frightened and nervous. I could be a very affectionate and faithful dog if only someone would be kind and give me a stable, loving home. Oh, and by the way, *I like cats.*'

The next day we were returning from the dog pound in Javea with Gesa in the back of the car, just hoping she had not lied on her CV.

Mickey's hackles rose and his fur bristled like a spiky punk rocker; his tail stood on end like a raccoon; his eyes bulged and he issued forth a kind of fiendish, wailing hiss as he stood on tip toes arching his back. And that was it. The pecking order was established and they were the best of friends, so long as Gesa minded her Ps and Qs, which she did by spending most of her first summer hiding under a bush in the garden. In every other respect she lived up to her blog, except that her name had to be changed. Gesa, pronounced with a gutteral German G, sounded like the noise you might make when clearing phlegm, so Gesa became Lisa.

The trouble with taking on an abandoned animal is that you never really know much about its upbringing or the events that have affected its personality or behaviour traits. As Lisa gradually gained confidence and responded to instructions, I decided to let her off her lead as we walked through the vineyards and the surrounding forest. All was fine for about three weeks; she never ventured too far away and always came back when called. Until one day she spotted a rabbit and chased it into the undergrowth. She returned eventually (without rabbit) and I was not too perturbed. Just two days later as we returned along a track at the side of the vineyards, Lisa disappeared into a clump of trees and started barking. Seconds later a small wild boar shot out of the trees, crossed the track and raced into the vineyards – followed by Lisa in hot pursuit. From our elevated position we watched the pair of them bob and weave through the vines and away into the far distance. As instructed by Viv, I, too, gave chase. It was forty minutes before Lisa finally emerged from a small patch of woodland on the far side of the valley. She was panting frantically, covered with sticky bobs and coated in black smelly mud – apart from that, she looked pretty pleased with herself. Her free roaming days were over, permanently.

With a new road to our house (courtesy of Vicente's son, the local councillor) our own concrete driveway was looking somewhat tired. It was crumbling and developing potholes of its own, so I decided to bite the bullet. My first thought was to buy in the materials, hire a concrete mixer and have a go myself. However, a rough calculation of the quantities required to cover an area of forty metres long by four metres wide (along with a bout of sciatica) led me to the conclusion that we needed a different solution in the form of one of the many concrete mixer wagons we frequently saw feeding local construction sites.

My first stop was Hocedesa, a large purveyor of building materials on the way to Benissa, where I had previously spotted a small fleet of concrete mixer wagons. In the office, the clerk explained that the wagons were owned by freelance drivers and I needed to contact one of them direct to arrange a delivery. Armed with the phone number for *Hormegon Francisco*, I made the call. It was all so easy. I explained that I wanted a lorry load of ready-mixed concrete to repair our drive and gave him directions to our hidden house. Francisco understood them perfectly, we agreed a price and the appointed time – eight o'clock the following Wednesday.

Now, pleasant as it was to be cared for by Nurse Viv, I did not want to repeat the experience of three weeks recuperating from a hernia operation. So I decided to enlist a little help in the form of my friend from Parcent, Mario, his brother Manolo and a couple of their mates. They, too, were scheduled to arrive at Finca Romero at eight o'clock on the appointed day. I congratulated myself; everything had been planned like a military operation.

Mario and crew arrived in good time armed with wheel barrows, shovels, rakes and planks. By five past eight there was no sign of Francisco, so I gave him a ring.

'I'm on my way. Just leaving Hocedesa and I'll be with you in five minutes.'

Great, the operation was going like clockwork.

Sure enough, Francisco arrived five minutes later – in his car.

'Where's the concrete?' I asked, wondering if the wagon was bringing up the rear.

Francisco was left to explain. He needed to inspect the job to determine the correct mix – the size of the gravel, the proportions of sand and cement and the liquidity of the mix. And there was me thinking concrete was just concrete. On top of that, I needed to sign an official order with my national identity number – in triplicate.

'But my crew are here now, ready and waiting.

What am I to do with them?'

'Send then for *almuerzo*,' Francisco said. 'I'll be back with the concrete in an hour.'

The cost of four breakfasts had just been added to the price of the job.

Apart from that little hiccup, Operation Concrete Driveway went relatively smoothly, except my initial calculations were somewhat optimistic and Francisco had to make two trips!

Chapter Thirteen

As the recession, or *La Crisis*, as it was called in Spain, began to bite we noticed subtle changes emerging in our valley. Several small shops closed for good and a number of well-established restaurants changed hands with new owners attempting (and often failing) to attract business. A net migration of expats left customers hard to find. Some restaurants began to offer what they called *Menu Crisis,* which made me wonder if this referred to the cost of the meal or the state of affairs in the kitchen. With employment hard to find and, for the Brits at least, the significant decline in the value of Sterling against the Euro, times were indeed hard.

If there was a silver lining it could be found in the fact that all those grandiose plans for vast new urbanisations were suddenly off the agenda. But that left the valley pock marked by unfinished construction sites and skeletal apartment blocks where work had ground to a halt. Once proudly adorned with hoardings announcing, '*Financiacion por Banco CAM,*' these sites were now effectively mothballed, waiting for better times to return. The banks' signs had been removed since they only served to illustrate the depth of their exposure to potentially toxic levels of debt. The *Vende* signs remained in place, but it seemed to me you would have to be a fool to invest in a half-finished development with no guarantee that it would ever be completed. The days when such apartments or villas were being bought "off plan" and sold like hot cakes were long gone – perhaps never to return.

Personally, I was quietly pleased that, for the foreseeable future, our valley would be saved further destruction. But there was a down-side. Many of our Spanish friends and neighbours were now struggling to find work. Boom to near bust is never easy, of course, but it seemed to me that most of my Spanish friends greeted the decline with a kind of philosophical stoicism. Many had seen hardship in the Franco years, as Spain's near isolation brought the economy virtually to its knees. Our nearest neighbour, Vicente, recalled the years in the fifties when he had shipped out to work for three months at a time in Switzerland, as the only way of supporting his family. And another friend, Josep, recounted the not so distant days gone by when the only meat on the table was that which he hunted himself, supplemented by herbs and plants which he foraged from the countryside.

I am sure it was different in the big conurbations like Madrid and Barcelona where street protests were a regular occurrence. And Valencia itself was struggling with a mountain of debt. It was hard to believe that not so long ago the powers-that-be had spent literally millions of euros to attract the Formula One Grand Prix and the America's Cup to Valencia. And yet now the local pharmacies were refusing to dispense prescription drugs because they had not been reimbursed by the Generalitat for more than six months. Education and public health services faced severe cutbacks, as did investment in new public infrastructure. All this was compounded by weekly newspaper reports about local, regional and national politicians who had been charged with corruption in one form or another and on a massive scale. Perhaps this, too, was a legacy of the Franco years, brushed under the carpet during the boom in tourism and construction, but now attracting the public's attention and rightful indignation.

The Jalon Valley was not immune from such hardships and had its fair share of political scandals. A former mayor of Lliber had been arrested for illegally approving the construction of more than two hundred houses dotted across the municipality. His fellow conspirator, the town hall architect, suffered a similar fate after a bank account containing more than a million euros was uncovered in Andorra. But as a predominantly rural area, the valley had a couple of things in its favour when it came to coping with *La Crisis*.

For most people, family life remained at the centre of everything; and unlike other regions where fractured relationships were almost the norm, most Spaniards hereabouts were able to fall back on their families for support. Many had resisted the temptation to sell-off village homes to the influx of northern Europeans. And, so it seemed to me, most people had not succumbed to the temptation of living beyond their means by taking on disproportionate burdens of debt. That is not to say that there were not hardships, especially for a younger generation who, just a few years earlier, might have expected job and career opportunities that had now all but evaporated.

Despite the hardships, most of Spain sticks rigidly

with tradition; siesta is sacrosanct. Even in the bigger towns and cities, most shops and banks still close at around one thirty and reopen at four or five o'clock. The 24/7 culture that predominates in most of northern Europe, is still eschewed in Spain and most shops are closed on Sundays. The many fiesta days, much more numerous than in the UK, are rigidly enforced with many businesses being instructed to close for the day, even if they don't want to. And unlike UK bank holiday Mondays, fiesta days are taken when they fall. So if May Day falls on a Thursday or All Saints' Day on a Tuesday, that's when the banks and shops close.

E-commerce is another area largely eschewed by many Spanish businesses. There are plenty of websites promoting companies large and small, but try to buy anything on-line and you are likely to hit a brick wall. I scoured the websites of several large electrical retailers and DIY stores in search of their best prices. All I found was a map directing me to my nearest store. A part of me felt this might be a good thing but, I am somewhat ashamed to admit, that did not stop me from using a couple of the major .co.uk retailers when everything else failed, especially since the cost of delivery was more than outweighed by the savings to be made.

No one enjoys paying taxes and people in Spain are no different. As tax residents in our adopted country, Viv and I conscientiously completed our annual tax returns within the requisite period. Of course, in harsh economic times the government needs all the money it can get. And yet, it seemed to me, payment of tax was often seen as a "voluntary" act and evasion was routine; compounded by a less than assiduous approach to scrutiny.

I'm no expert, so these comments are based on my personal experience. When buying building materials, I was routinely asked if I wanted a receipt. If I answered in the negative, then IVA (the Spanish equivalent of VAT at 21%) was omitted from the cost. In one such establishment, I had collected several items of guttering, downspouts, connectors and clips. The items were totalled up in the office and, when I produced a credit card to pay, the female assistant said, 'Ah, I thought you would be paying in cash so I have not included IVA.'

The point is that I was a stranger in this place, not a regular, and yet they were happy to offer me this "facility". Presumably, I surmised, I must look honest and trustworthy and not the least bit like a Spanish tax inspector.

One Saturday morning, I called in at another outlet, a large retailer of smart bathrooms, Jacuzzis and swimming pool paraphernalia. All I wanted was a large tub of chlorine for the pool, but when I presented this at the counter along with my credit card, the friendly man said, 'Could you pay in cash? It's just that I only work here on Saturdays and I don't know how to operate the computer. There's no IVA if you have the cash.'

Well, we all like a bargain, don't we? I later discovered that the friendly shop assistant was in fact the owner of the business – and in his spare time he was the mayor of that particular town. I came to know him quite well when I visited his shop on other occasions – always on a Saturday!

Political Correctness is another area where Spain has failed to keep up. Or, more likely, has consciously shunned modern trends. Take for example the *Moros y Cristianos* festivals that feature annually in many towns across the region and often last for a whole week. Participants, many with blackened faces, re-enact the many battles between the Muslims and Christians in the Middle Ages. In sumptuous costumes and following elaborate rituals, thousands of people celebrate the eventual re-conquest of Spain with a simulated battle for a castle that always ends in defeat for the Moors. Perhaps Britain could follow suit with a celebration of the Crusades!

And as for Health and Safety? All I can say is that "Claims 4U" would struggle to get established in Spain, even on a "No win – No fee" basis.

So these are my modest reflections on Spain and the Spanish people. How might I sum them up? Relaxed, friendly, tolerant, practical, helpful. These are all adjectives I would readily apply. There were a few expats I talked to who recounted tales of surliness, bad manners and outright prejudice, but I can honestly say that (with the exception of the driver of the oil tanker and my political skirmishes in Parcent) I never encountered anything of this nature. I did wonder if this was because I had become more Spanish myself and had adjusted to the Spanish way of doing things. Though there may be some truth in this, the more likely explanation is this: when you live in a place where the sun shines for three hundred days a year and the rain is viewed as a blessing, it is easy to wake up and start each day in a positive frame of mind. And if you approach the people you encounter with the same degree of cheerfulness and optimism, you will generally find it is reciprocated, especially if you make an effort to learn their language.

This much was true of Vicente and Pepita next door. I am sure they thought us indolent as we existed without gainful employment in contrast to their hard working regimes. Vicente, now in his early seventies, could be seen most mornings puttering off into the distance on his *mula mecánica* to tend a plot of olives or almonds or grapes. Pepita fulfilled her role as housewife, mother and grandmother, still following the pattern of the patriarchal model propounded under Franco and underpinned by the Catholic Church. I am sure she found it strange that I shopped and cooked, since these were tasks strictly within a woman's realm.

At busy times of the year, Pepita would also lend a hand harvesting the grapes, setting out the olives to dry or cracking hard almond shells. Though Vicente kept three or four dogs (I was never sure exactly how many) these were strictly for hunting and kept hidden away in kennels at the back of his house. I know for certain that he thought us barmy for even allowing our animals to enter the house; and what he would have said had he known about their sleeping arrangements is anyone's guess. I had the greatest difficulty explaining why I had picked a crop of under-ripe peas when I presented him with a bagful of mange tout. And when I answered his polite enquiry as to where I went every morning in the car by explaining I was collecting a daily English newspaper, it only confirmed to him that we were truly eccentric, not to say profligate. However, these simple differences never got in the way of our friendship, but that is not to say that we truly understood each other's way of life.

On Sundays and fiesta days Pepita would regularly cater for her extended family when a crowd of twenty plus arrived. Occasionally I enquired as to what was on the menu. Almost always the answer was rice of some description and of course paella. She often presented us with homemade *cocas*, like minis pizzas with toppings of peas, tomato or sliced chorizo, and at Christmas we exchanged our homemade mince pies for sweetmeats made from ground almonds and *calabaza* (pumpkin).

There was great excitement at Pepita's house one Sunday morning – the yard had been swept, windows cleaned and a long table set in the naya. I asked what was happening and Pepita explained that a cousin of hers from Pedreguer had recently harvested his crop of potatoes. This, by itself, was unusual as I had never seen potatoes growing hereabouts.

'We're having a potato fiesta,' Pepita said, 'and all the family will be round for lunch.'

'And what will you be cooking?' I asked.

She gave me a quizzical look. 'Potatoes,' she said.

'But what else... to go with the potatoes?' I enquired.

Her quizzical look turned to a frown. 'Nothing, just potatoes. That's why it's called a potato fiesta.'

Later that day, Pepita presented us with a dish of *patatas del pobre* – poor man's potatoes. They were delicious, a bit like the French Boulangère potatoes, just layers of thinly sliced potatoes slowly baked in a shallow tray with a little olive oil and stock, lashings of garlic and a sprinkling of parsley. Sometimes the simplest of dishes really are the best.

One of my oft-used pieces of home-spun philosophy is that life doesn't just present itself on a plate – you have to make a life for yourself wherever you live and whatever serendipity or misfortune comes your way. The upshot of living by this maxim is that when you take a decision you have to stick with it. There's no going back, so you might as well just get on with it.

And though life was good for both of us, Viv's main regret was the distance from her father, Ben, who lived in the north west of England, not far from Manchester airport. Regular trips home were scant compensation for Viv, and this was compounded by Ben's reluctance to travel to Spain. His age was one excuse, as was his fear of leaving his house empty for any length of time. Added to that was Ben's professed fear of flying, which I always found hard to understand given that he had served in World War II as a wireless operator and navigator in the RAF. In between visits, Viv and Ben would talk by telephone virtually every day – sometimes for hours – and in a curious way, I think they actually became closer despite the distance between them.

It was a sixth sense, I am sure, but when Ben failed to answer several phone calls one Saturday afternoon, Viv knew in her heart what had happened. Like my old friend Willie, Ben had been diagnosed with an aneurysm some years before. The medical advice was that an operation would present more of a risk than trying to maintain the situation by means of regular check-ups. Ben often talked of having a ticking time-bomb in his body, but he was sanguine about his situation as he approached his eighty-seventh birthday. Even so, his death came as a devastating blow to Viv who will always regret not being with her father and not being able to say goodbye. And the echo of those unspoken words would reverberate through Viv's daily thoughts, diminishing with time, but never fading away.

We had returned to Spain after Ben's funeral just the day before when Viv's attention was caught by a movement in the garden. 'Mark, quick come outside,' she said, 'I swear I've just seen a dog in the garden.' It was pitch-black and a thorough search turned up nothing. I went to bed wondering if Viv had taken one glass of wine too many.

The next morning, I wandered around the back of the house to the site of our old ruin and caught a glimpse of something moving amidst the rubble. Sure enough, there he was; a tiny, scrawny, motley scruff of a dog. He cowered as I approached and presented himself in a submissive pose as I picked him up. Viv was still in the house and for a fleeting moment I thought about opening the gate of the ruin plot to show him the way out. But I relented and carried the tick- and flea-ridden creature to the house. Within moments Viv was busy with the old insecticidal shampoo (and the tweezers) and he emerged with the canine equivalent of a perfumed curly perm. He spent his first night shivering in the corner on an old blanket, declining all offers of food despite his emaciated state. We both began to fear he would not see the night out. After a full inspection and a couple of jabs, the vet confirmed he was a pure bred Breton

Spaniel around six months old and the anomalous absence of a tail was a naturally occurring phenomenon. I found it hard to believe this dog had any pedigree whatsoever. He was a curious mix of colours – grey with every shade of brown from beige to chocolate. His fur was patterned in blotches and spots of colour with speckles on his legs. His coat ranged from straight and silky, to coarse and wiry, to tangled curls. There were a number of design faults as well. His eyes were a bright gold and accentuated by long eyelashes, one set white, the other brown. His floppy spaniel ears, covered in long wavy fur, fluttered about his head like the flaps on a Sherlock Holmes deerstalker, and it was impossible for him to take a drink without getting them wet. In short, he was a badly drawn boy.

He had been close to death, the vet said, and it was his good fortune to have found us just in time. He had no microchip and if we wanted to chip him and register him, he was as good as ours. I resisted on the grounds that he might already belong to someone else, but I should have known better.

'You've seen the state of him,' Viv said. 'If he belongs to someone else, they don't deserve him.'

A gift? A reincarnation? Who knows? Benji had arrived. Despite escaping through the gates on a couple of occasions (he was thin enough to squeeze through the bars) he quickly realised on which side his bread had been buttered. Being just a puppy, he was more incautious than Lisa when it came to knowing his place, but he soon got the message – 'Don't mess with Mickey.' Even so, his antics led us to give him the nickname *Pesadilla* which translates as 'Nightmare' and pretty much summed up the next few months of our lives. So, you see, you really do have to live with the consequences of your decisions – if only I had just opened that gate…

An English friend, Kate, whom I first met at Spanish classes, kindly invited us for a paella lunch at her house on the edge of Lliber. I call it a house, but in fact it was a small complex designed and built as a kind of mini resort. As well as the main house, equipped with a full-sized catering kitchen and entertaining rooms, there were ten en-suite letting rooms for paying guests. It was a splendid place surrounded by an extensive plot of land which was home to several rescued donkeys, innumerable cats and dogs and a pair of Vietnamese pot-bellied pigs – all the result of Kate's inability to resist the call of any waif or stray she encountered.

A small aside is due here, before I return to the paella – on the subject of the pot-bellied pigs. When I first encountered them I couldn't help noticing that the smaller of the two appeared pregnant with its teats hanging full and large and virtually dragging on the ground.

'When are the piglets due?' I asked.

Kate looked shocked. 'You don't really think she is pregnant, do you?'

'Well, I'm no vet, but have you seen her? She looks pretty pregnant to me.'

'Oh, no,' Kate said. 'That would be a disaster.'

'But why?' I asked. 'In a few months time you could have a ready supply of bacon, albeit in tiny rashers.'

Kate was now looking seriously distressed. 'Because I've had them for six months and the big one is the father of the little one!'

Back to the paella. There were more than forty guests, mainly Spanish, seated at a long table in the shade of the naya on a gloriously sunny June day. Someone had brought along an acoustic guitar and entertained us with a selection of flamenco music which prompted some of the guests to demonstrate their dancing flair.

Everyone seemed happy and relaxed, including Kate and I did wonder why there was no flurry of activity in the kitchen. Right on cue, a van pulled up in front of the house with the logo, "Restaurante Val de Pop," the place where I had sampled the *fideuá* just a few months before. The driver began unloading six large dishes of paella, placing them at intervals along the table. Everyone tucked in and with the music, the dancing, the wine and the general bonhomie around the table, it was a truly splendid Spanish occasion. And the paella? It was excellent, very authentic and very tasty indeed. Above all, it was quite a spectacle topped symmetrically with halved red peppers and with wedges of lemon tucked neatly around the perimeter. The whole dish reminded me of the colours of the Spanish flag.

Contented and quite merry, I wondered for a while if my pursuit of the perfect paella had finally come to an end. But then it occurred to me. From its inception, my quest had been fatally flawed. For there is no such thing as a perfect paella – only a perfect paella occasion. It's a dish meant to be shared with friends, and if you are lucky enough to leave an empty *paellera,* replete and with a sense of warm-hearted friendliness and conviviality, then you, too, may have encountered the perfect paella occasion.

*****

So that's it, the end of my quest. If I've captured your imagination or whetted your appetite for Spain, or just for paella, then my purpose has been fulfilled. If you read this book out of sequence, you may care to discover more about our early years in Spain in my first book I want to live in Spain @ Amazon.co.uk And below you'll find details of my other books. Finally, if you care to give it a try, there's a recipe for paella at the end of this book and some tips on buying property in Spain.

BY THE SAME AUTHOR

MISSING IN SPAIN

A compelling murder mystery featuring Detective Inspector Fernandez.
A British couple disappear in Spain and as a fluent Spanish speaker, British detective Michael Fernandez seems the ideal choice to help track them down. But he finds more than he bargained for when he encounters a branch of his family he had previously tried to forget. Then a body is found and the hunt for the killer is on.

"An excellent read for those who like detective stories. Read from cover to cover in a couple of days, would have been less, but life interfered. A complex, brisk plot with lots of side interest. I hope this will only be the first of many outings for Inspector Michael Fernandez."

SPANISH LIES

Detective Inspector Fernandez returns to Spain to investigate a tangled web of murder, corruption and immorality on the Costa Blanca. Meanwhile, in the village where he has inherited a home, the tentacles of local life engulf him in an irresistible intrigue and a mystery that has its roots in the aftermath of the Spanish Civil War.

"This is an excellent detective novel with lots of twists and turns to keep you thinking right to the end! Just the right balance between the plot and background of the main character's private life. Really enjoyed it!"

A SPANISH AFFRAY

The third Fernandez novel. When the body of a British ex-con is fished from the Mediterranean, Michael Fernandez is once again called on to investigate. Now a captain in the Guardia Civil, Michael must face his own doubts and demons as he unravels a case that leads him back to an unsolved robbery and murder from ten years earlier. His pursuit of one of "Britain's Most Wanted" takes him to the limit of his powers but he refuses to back off. But what motivates him to put his own future on the line when a desperate situation gets out of hand?

"After reading the first of the Michael Fernandez series and enjoying it immensely I went straight onto reading books two and three and neither disappointed. I like the area of Spain in which they

are set and the Spanish family background and customs provide an interesting aside to the underlying crime story. Mark Harrison doesn't fall into the trap of over complicating or lengthening the stories which made them an enjoyable read for me. I hope that the sequel isn't too long in being released."

A LASTING PACT

In the immediate aftermath of the Spanish Civil War, General Franco seeks to strengthen his tenuous grip on power by suppressing and eliminating all opposition whether real or imagined. Under this guise, Eduardo Ripoll finds himself unjustly imprisoned in the village of Benimarta.

When Eduardo is taken away in the middle of the night and consigned to prison in Alicante, Vicenta embarks on a perilous journey to find him – a journey made more difficult by the knowledge she is now pregnant. Unable to support herself in the city, Vicenta is forced to rely on the *Auxilio Social* run by the *Sección Femenina* of the *Falange Español* and endure its authoritarian regime.

When her son, Reny, is born in traumatic circumstances, Vicenta must fight for his survival and her right to motherhood. With Eduardo still missing, she returns to Benimarta with a plan to secure Reny's future, free from the threat of abduction or internment. As the years pass and Reny matures, Eduardo is never far from Vicenta's thoughts. She refuses to accept that Eduardo is dead and she can never forget or forgive the injustice he has suffered.

Finally the truth is revealed and Vicenta is

presented with an opportunity – if not for justice, then for revenge.

"A well researched novel, well written and with carefully developed characters. It has a spellbinding storyline with deep descriptive passages which create a smouldering effect. Also some quite brutal and action-packed sections which increase the pace. The dialogue is clear and concise, quite clipped and snappy. There is good background information and the novel draws you in very early on. A sense of time and place are created from the first page. There is atmosphere and tension and emotional impact. Well worth a read."

A Recipe for Paella

Like most things in life, you can have too much of a good thing, and so paella events should really be saved for special occasions. However, this created a problem as it had become one of my favourite meals. It wasn't just eating paella that I enjoyed; I had become enthralled with the process of preparing the enigmatic dish. It wasn't simply the act of putting the ingredients together that interested me; I was fascinated by the cooking process itself. Cooking paella involves alchemy – a seemingly magical process of transformation, creating a finished dish which is somehow much more sophisticated than the mere sum of its ingredients. And this led me to another eureka moment – even cooked from the same recipe, no two paellas are ever the same. There are just too many variables – temperature, the type of rice, the quality of the oil, the size of and composition of the pan, the choice of meat and fish, even the source of the water used for stock – all these have an impact on the final outcome. But don't be put off by this, for the best (if not the perfect) paella is always the one you cook yourself and if you fancy giving it a try here's my recipe. But first a word of explanation. Like so many sentimental Brits, Viv would never eat rabbit and, again like so many others, she has an aversion to chewing meat off bones. So a few adaptations were necessary right from the outset which makes this probably the least authentic paella it is possible to imagine. So, with apologies to Lina of Bar Varetes and every other Spanish housewife, here is my recipe for "Viv's not so Valencian Paella."

Serves two people.

You will need a large (12 inch) non-stick frying pan (unless you just happen to have a small *paellera* hanging in the kitchen).

Ingredients.

3 boneless chicken thighs cut into cubes
8 large uncooked whole prawns
A three-inch piece of chorizo sliced
8 runner beans cut into one-inch slices
A small red pepper, sliced and cut into chunks
2 cloves of garlic, peeled and roughly chopped
A good pinch of chili flakes
A good pinch of saffron
1 mug of paella rice (definitely not long grain rice)
3 mugs of hot chicken stock (preferably home-made though a cube would do)
Olive oil
1 lemon cut into wedges

Method

1. Place the saffron in a small bowl and add a little boiling water, set aside.
2. Peel half the prawns and cut them in half, saving the shells. Reserve the remaining four prawns for later.
3. Place the prawn shells in a small pan with a little of the stock and bring to the boil for a couple of minutes. Discard the prawn shells and return the stock to the remainder.
4. Add a little olive oil to the frying pan and cook

the pepper until soft and slightly charred. Set aside in a large bowl. Repeat with the sliced runner beans and set aside in the same bowl.

5. In the same frying pan, cook the chorizo for one minute over gentle heat until it has released its red oils. Place in the bowl leaving the chorizo oil in the pan.
6. Cook the chicken pieces in the frying pan over medium heat until lightly browned. Place in the bowl.
7. Now place the rice in the frying pan with a little olive oil and heat until all the rice grains are coated.
8. Add all the stock and bring to a boil over high heat, stirring occasionally. Continue to boil for 10 minutes then add the saffron and its liquid and the chili flakes.
9. Next add all the ingredients from the bowl (meat, chorizo, peppers, beans, prawn pieces and chicken) together with the chopped garlic. Stir once to distribute all the ingredients, season with a little salt and continue to cook over high heat. Important – do not stir again.
10. Place the unpeeled prawns on top of the paella and press down lightly.
11. Now is the critical stage. After about ten minutes the pan will cease to bubble and start to sizzle as the stock is absorbed by the rice. Continue cooking for a few more minutes until the "*socarrat*" (the crispy brown layer at the bottom of the pan) has formed. Do not stir, but you can lift a small portion of the paella to check that the bottom is beginning to turn brown and crispy.

12. Finally turn off the heat and allow the paella to stand for a minute or two. Distribute the lemon wedges around the edge of the pan and move to the table to serve.
Enjoy.

Notes.
If you would like a more "fishy" paella, you could add a few mussels as well and perhaps some squid. If you are cooking for more than two people just increase the ingredients accordingly. The important thing to remember is to use three mugs of stock to every mug of rice. It may seem a lot, but don't worry, it will all be absorbed by the rice. You will need a bigger pan – paella simply will not cook properly if it is more than an inch thick.

And finally... I have been accused of wearing rose tinted spectacles when it comes to living in Spain. There's probably some truth in that as I continue to be beguiled by my adopted homeland. If you have been inspired to consider Spain either as a place to live or to visit or to buy a holiday home, here are a few things to consider.

Ten Good Reasons to Live in Spain

1. The weather - we get 300 days of sunshine in the Costa Blanca every year.

2. The people - the Spanish people are generally welcoming and friendly.

3. The weather - maximum temperatures in summer rarely exceed 38C. Mornings and evenings are generally cooler.

4. The cost of living - whilst the cost of most things is generally on a par with the UK, local taxes are considerably lower at an average of around 400 euros a year including rubbish collection. Compare this with UK council tax.

5. The weather - it is a little too hot for two months and a little too cold for two months, but the rest of the year (that's eight months) the weather is perfect.

6. There are plenty of good bars and restaurants and you can still eat out for 12 – 15 euros including wine - and the price of a pint is around 2.50 euros (a bit more on the coast).

7. The weather - you can barbeque in January and eat outdoors at lunchtime for most of the winter (when the sun shines).

8. The pace of life - everyone is very laid back. OK so the *manana* culture can be frustrating at times, but it's rare to see a traffic jam.

9. The weather - OK so it rains sometimes, but it tends to come in big dollops and the sunshine is always quick to return.

10. I've been in Spain for more than 12 years now and I wouldn't want to live anywhere else.

Ten things that might deter people from enjoying life in Spain

1. Bureaucracy. I've mentioned it already, but Spain really is the form-filling capital of Europe. And just when you think you have all the paperwork you need, the person who asked for it will think of something else.

2. Disruptions to public services. One look at the ancient cables strung to the outside of properties with exposed junction boxes and you will understand why rain or storms frequently result in power cuts. Water supplies, too, suffer cuts, and don't expect advance notice when planned maintenance takes place.

3. Unscrupulous agents and property developers. Sad to say there are still plenty of rogues out there eager to make a fast buck and leave buyers in the lurch. It's not helped by regional governments who have consistently failed to protect buyers and yet insist that buying in Spain is "safe." The pitfalls are avoidable, but you need to be careful. (See my tips below).

4. Noise. Spain is a noisy country and at almost every event – birthdays, weddings, fiestas – you can expect loud music and fireworks. The Spanish people are generally more tolerant of this than expats might be, and the effect is exaggerated by the weather and the outdoor lifestyle. But it's not just the Spaniards that cause the problem. Partying expats can be just as noisy either at home or in late night bars and clubs. And I won't mention barking dogs.

5. Untidiness. Spain has some beautiful countryside, but it's not uncommon to see it spoiled by discarded litter. I just don't think the Spanish people notice it so much. Roadside verges are frequently untended and littered with discarded bottles, cans and building debris.

6. Slow service. Spaniards just don't seem to do things in a hurry. Gossiping with friends in front of a queue of people is not uncommon, and if the phone rings this will always take precedence over waiting customers.

7. Lack of choice. This one's for Viv who frequently bemoans the lack of choice in shops (for clothes, but not for shoes) and in supermarkets (especially for ready-made meals). If only Marks and Spencer had an outlet nearby!

8. The language barrier. You can (and should) learn basic Spanish to get by, or go a little further

as I have, but even so, it is always going to be difficult to deal with complicated problems or medical issues without help from an interpreter.

9. The weather. Yes, the sun shines more often than not and that's why people love Spain. But twelve weeks of unrelenting summer sun is very different from a two week vacation. We are always pleased to see the onset of autumn. Then again, winter can be cold. Snow and frost are not uncommon, in the mountains if not on the coast. If you plan to winter in Spain, think seriously about how you are going to keep warm.

10. Prices. Wine and eating out are generally cheaper than in the UK. Local taxes are much cheaper as well. In supermarkets, most items are on a par with the UK, though some are more expensive. However, fuel bills are much more expensive, as is broadband. And if you plan to become tax resident in Spain, expect to pay more in personal taxation.

My top ten tips to avoid disasters when buying property in Spain.

1. Always engage the services of a good lawyer, but never use a lawyer recommended by an estate agent. Remember, the estate agent through whom you buy is paid by the vendor. He/she may offer all kinds of help and advice, but their principal purpose is to act in the interests of the seller and

secure their fee. Don't be fooled into thinking the agent is your friend.

2. Take your time. When you've found your dream home it's easy to get carried away. If an agent tries to rush the process, be suspicious. Never pay a deposit without first consulting a lawyer.

3. Don't do anything you wouldn't do at home. Some people assume Spain is free and easy, but if you plan to extend your home in the future or build a pool, you need to check with the town hall before you buy – and Spain leads the world in bureaucracy. Don't believe anyone who says: 'Just build and pay the fine later.'

4. Think twice about buying a new property off-plan. Can you be sure that if you hand over a deposit, the property will actually be completed? The deposit may be refundable, but that doesn't mean you will get your money back if things go wrong. Similarly if there are communal facilities to be built – like a communal pool or gardens – can you be sure they will ever be finished, and who will pay for on-going maintenance?

5. Check the status of the property to make sure it is fully legal. The best way to do this is to ask your lawyer to get an *Informe Urbanistico* (Urbanistic Report) from the town hall. This will show the zoning of the land and state whether there have been any infringements of planning

rules. Get your lawyer to ask specifically if there is any new development planned in the vicinity of your home. Also check that the property has a *Cedula de Habitabilidad.* (Sometimes called a licence of primary or secondary occupation). This certificate confirms that everything has been built correctly and the house is fully legal. Finally check that the house has proper contracts for services – water, electricity and telephone – always ask to see the bills. Be very wary if any of these services are shared with neighbours or on a temporary (or builder's) supply. Public utility companies will not enter into a permanent contract unless the property has all the correct paperwork from the town hall.

6. Your lawyer will check the land registry to be sure there are no outstanding debts on the property. (In Spain, debts if not cleared before sale, pass on to the new owners). Make sure the lawyer also checks the local land registry (*Catastro*) which will show what is actually registered as built on the land and set the basis for local taxes.

7. Watch out for urbanisations with unfinished roads, footpaths, street lighting or sewers. If the urbanisation is not finished properly and adopted by the town hall, the future costs of this infrastructure may eventually fall on the residents and could run into thousands of euros.

8. At the end of the process you will go to the Notary to sign the *Escritura* (Deeds). Don't assume that the Notary is certifying the legality of the deal. The Notary is little more than a public witness to the transaction and bears no responsibility if things go wrong.

9. For years there has been a practice of undervaluing the stated purchase price of a property in the *Escritura* in order to reduce taxes. Although this practice is less common now, it still goes on. But be warned, the authorities are tightening up and there can be serious financial consequences for the purchaser even several years after the sale.

10. Don't listen to gossip. All manner of home-spun advice is readily on offer in bars and restaurants – most of it false or misleading. Ignore it. If you have any doubts about anything, talk to your lawyer and press him/her to give you proper advice in writing. And if you still have doubts don't listen to anyone who says: 'Don't worry about it, this is just the way things are done in Spain.'

And finally – don't be put off by this; just exercise due diligence and you should be able to avoid the pitfalls.

END

Printed in Great Britain
by Amazon